HARDWIRING EXCELLENCE

PURPOSE

WORTHWHILE WORK

MAKING A DIFFERENCE

QUINT STUDER

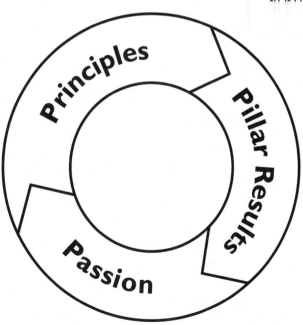

COPYRIGHT INFORMATION

"Quint has done what psychologists have said could never be done. He invented the engineering for hardwiring positive attitudes in hospitals that transform cultures and subsequently improve fiscal outcomes."

Jim Clifton
Chairman and CEO
The Gallup Organization

*"I read **Hardwiring Excellence** with great interest and admiration. It is easy to forget about the human side of health care. Quint's book is a real wake-up call and provides health care leaders with the very tools and ideas to be successful."*

Professor Regina E. Herzlinger
Nancy R. McPherson Professor of Business Administration
Harvard Business School

*"Quint Studer is transforming health care through a national revolution that begins with an employee-centered culture. **Hardwiring Excellence** is the ultimate guide for the journey to becoming a world-class organization."*

Debbie Cardello, MSN, RN, CHE
Chief Operating Officer
Robert Wood Johnson University Hospital, Hamilton, NJ

*"**Hardwiring Excellence** is unmatched in its ability to provide a step-by-step guide to sustainable improvement. It's a gift of heartwarming stories, humorous insights, and laserbeam focus on how to make a positive difference —for employees, physicians, and customers."*

Michael W. Murphy
President & CEO
Sharp HealthCare, San Diego, CA

"A Must Read for every CNO and nurse leader. Quint Studer maps the path from dream to reality . . . hospitals where patients receive superior care and clinicians are valued in the way we have always deserved to be. It's all about the power of people to transform health care as we know it."

Linda Deering, RN, MSN
Vice President & Chief Nursing Officer
Delnor-Community Hospital, Geneva, IL

"For every physician who wants to spend more time caring for patients and less time resolving complaints. I finally believe my ability to reward and recognize the 'exceptionally normal' in colleagues now matches my professional training in how to diagnose the abnormal in patients. Thank you, Quint Studer."

Bill Colgate, M.D.
Medical Director, Emergency Care Center
Sarasota Memorial Hospital, Sarasota, FL

"At last, a resource for finance leaders on how to create a dialogue at all levels of the organization that standardizes strong leadership, drives employee ownership for financial performance, and shares what we can learn from front-line employees who affect our financials on a daily basis."

Jim Beck
Chief Financial Officer
All Saints Healthcare, Racine, WI

"I think the silo effect in health care often prevents good communication between nursing and ancillary departments to best serve patients. With coaching by Studer Group, we now have a culture where nurses and dietary staff take joint ownership for process improvement. When food scores on a med-surg unit dipped recently, instead of blaming, we added chicken soup to the menu and began rounding with a second drinks cart between meals so nurses could focus on caregiving."

Larry Pizzorni, CEC, CCE
System Director, Food and Nutrition
Blue Ridge HealthCare, Morganton, NC

DEDICATION

To Fire Starters Everywhere

• Prescriptive
  To Do's

Principles

Pillar Results

Purpose
Worthwhile
Work and
Making
a Difference

• Results Tied
  to Each Pillar

Passion

• Self-Motivation

**HARDWIRING
EXCELLENCE**

TABLE OF CONTENTS

TABLE OF CONTENTS

FOREWORD

W hen I speak at health care conferences my keynote address frequently follows a futurist or two. Their talks go something like this: First, they show a graph with a line going up (that's the aging baby boomer population that will need more and more of our resources in health care).

Then they show another line going up—that's the cost of providing health care, rising due to the increasing cost of new drugs and technology. Then there are the lines that go down because caregivers will be more scarce and reimbursement more challenging.

In short, they show compelling statistics for the "Perfect Storm" that's brewing in health care—projected to hit around 2010 or so—and walk off the stage to thunderous applause, because what can we really do?

This book is about what we can do. I believe we are at the tipping point in health care. Will we feed the national crisis or bring solutions?

I elected to publish the first edition of *Hardwiring Excellence* in paperback, instead of hardcover, to keep the cost low, for it is my greatest hope that every leader will read it and then ask those who work with them to read it too.

FOREWORD

I hope the stories and prescriptive tools offered within these pages inspire you and your organization to reach high on your journey to hardwiring excellence—just as so many people whom I work with have inspired me to feel purpose, worthwhile work, and making a difference. This keeps my flame alive.

As Ferdinand Foche, French Allied Supreme Commander in World War I, said, *"The greatest force on earth is the human soul on fire."*

- Prescriptive To Do's

Principles

Pillar Results

- Results Tied to Each Pillar

Purpose Worthwhile Work and Making a Difference

Passion

- Self-Motivation

HARDWIRING EXCELLENCE

INTRODUCTION

Blessed is the influence of one true loving human soul on another. — George Eliot

I know this book begins with my story, but it's not about me. Or the success of any particular hospital where I have worked. Or even the tools I once used in those hospitals. They have changed a great deal since those days, because I have integrated the best practices at hundreds of organizations into what Studer Group℠ recommends today.

No, this book is really about you and your commitment to hardwiring excellence. And at the very heart of the journey are passion and caring.

I remember one day in October 2002 when I received a note of apology from Dr. Floyd Loop, CEO, of the Cleveland Clinic Foundation. He was sorry, he said, to have missed our meeting, but life had gotten in the way.

Dr. Loop, a world-renowned surgeon, spent the day at the bedside of his best friend, who was dying. Dr. Loop explained:

> *Al said to me, "I'm not going easy, and I don't want you to leave me."*
>
> *So I held his hand for five and one half hours until he died at 8:30 p.m. that evening.*
>
> *He was my best friend and the embodiment of courage, leadership, humanity, and patriotism. He managed me up for more than 10 years.*

Like thousands of Fire Starters in health care today, Dr. Loop is a leader who understands the influence of one true loving human soul on another.

My wish is for you, too, to feel its power.

HARDWIRING
EXCELLENCE

CHAPTER ONE

MY JOURNEY TO BECOMING A FIRE STARTER

While I may have ended up as a hospital president in 1996, my journey into health care was a little bit unusual. And I think those experiences helped me to understand the power of individuals who make a difference in the lives of others. I call them Fire Starters. Today, I am fortunate to work with thousands of difference-makers who are committed to transforming health care through compassion, imagination, and often, sheer determination. This book is my tribute to these Fire Starters.

But let me start at the beginning. When I was a child, I had a rough time academically. In fact, I'm not sure I would have survived school at all if it hadn't been for three very special teachers who believed in me: Mrs. James, Mr. Fry, and Mr. King.

I was not a good student. I couldn't speak very well because I had a speech impediment. I still couldn't read by the end of the second grade. In fact, I'm pretty sure the only reason they agreed to promote me to third grade at all was because my mother was the vice president of the PTA.

By the time I was nine years old, I already knew I was a reject. I couldn't stay in my own classroom all day like the other kids. I was pulled out for speech therapy. *But Mrs. James, my third grade teacher, made a difference in my life.* I can't tell you exactly what she did, but I would take risks for her that I would never take for any other teacher. She even invited me to stand up at the front of the room and perform in a skit once. It was the first time in my life a teacher had done that, because people couldn't understand me. It just didn't come naturally. But Mrs. James set me up to succeed. She found a few words I could say: "I'm as poor as ever." She even had me visualize pouring milk so that I could say the word *poor. I felt like I was important.* Today, I call it feeling worthwhile. I never would have believed then that eventually I would have the confidence to spend many of my days speaking in front of large groups as I do now. This is why I often talk about the importance of worthwhile work and making a difference in health care.

My sixth-grade teacher was Mr. Fry. What I liked about Mr. Fry was that he always looked for the positive. While other teachers told my mother that I couldn't sit still, Mr. Fry said, "Quint really has *energy!*" Other teachers complained that I couldn't focus. Mr. Fry said he was impressed by my ability to "multitask." He made a point of noticing what was right, not what was wrong. I think it's because of Mr. Fry that I urge health care leaders to ingrain (or "hardwire") systems and tools that recognize what's right and what's working well.

Later, when I went to high school, I decided to play soccer because it was the only sport where they didn't cut anybody. My soccer coach Mr. King had a way of correcting me without destroying me. He would come up to me and say, "Quint, way to hustle! Way to get to that ball!" Then, almost as an afterthought, he'd add, "Next time, *let's put the foot out.* But hey, you got there! Way to go!"

You know how I felt? Pretty good. I had hustled. I had gotten there. And the next time, you better believe that I remembered to put my foot out. What if he had said, "Quint! What's the matter with you? What good does it do for you to run all that way if you don't kick the ball? Sit down now so I can put somebody else in."

I might have run a little slower the next time to make sure I didn't get yelled at for missing the ball. Coach King taught me to go for the ball. If we only hear about what we can't do, it seems easier to give up. Many of us do. In fact, of the people who leave their jobs at a health care organization, a great many leave within the first 90 days. About 27 percent of all employees who leave do so during this early period of employment. They don't leave to go work in some other industry. They just give up on their current health care employer and try another one. I believe this is because they hear too much about what they can't do instead of what they can do.

In 1969, I graduated from high school with a 1.3 GPA. Although college didn't look like much of an option, my friends talked me into taking the ACT with them. I did better on the test than anybody expected, and people at school started thinking that maybe I wasn't as dumb as my grades made me look. They began looking for a college that would accept me.

I ended up at the University of Wisconsin-Whitewater, a college that took time to help students like me. And after a couple of years, I had earned a 2.5 GPA. While other guys would have been killed for having those grades, that was a significant achievement for me. My dad thought I was a rocket scientist.

When the time came to choose a major, I thought of the three people who had had the greatest impact on my life: Mrs. James, Mr. Fry, and Mr. King. I made up my mind to become a teacher.

In 1973, I graduated and became a special education teacher like Mr. King. Five years later, I got a Master's degree because I wanted to be the best teacher I could be. I taught special education for over 10 years.

One of the most rewarding periods in my special ed career was when I taught vocational education for students ages 14 to 21. A big part of my teaching role was getting jobs for my students. Barb was one of them. She worked at McDonald's making malts from 1:30 to 3:00 p.m. when McDonald's wasn't busy. She always wore her McDonald's uniform to school on the days when she would work. But one day she wore her uniform on a day when she wasn't scheduled to work. I thought she was confused and told her she didn't need to wear it on those days.

But I found out she wasn't confused at all. Barb knew she felt better about herself on the days when she wore that uniform. She understood what worthwhile work does to a person and how it makes her feel about herself. She felt that other students looked at her differently when she wore the uniform. She was not "apart from," but "a part of." I believe all employees want to feel "a part of." Purpose, worthwhile work, and making a difference evoke that feeling.

MY START IN HEALTH CARE

Over time, I became aware of a new position at a small 35-bed substance abuse hospital that helped kids and adults with alcohol and drug problems. They were seeking a community relations representative to act as liaison between the school district, area employers, and the center. Since I knew a number of students who had been treated there, I had a keen interest in their work.

They appreciated my interest, along with some community recognition I had received (Outstanding Young Educator of the Year by the Janesville Jaycees and Outstanding Educator by the Rock County Association of Retarded Citizens). So they offered me the job, and I worked for Parkside Lodge of Janesville, Wisconsin, for three years. I liked the feeling of that hospital and how they helped put lives back together. It was worthwhile work.

I remember a particular day at the hospital when I answered the phone for a nurse who was busy with a patient in detox. While I didn't normally answer the phones, at a small hospital there is really no such thing as "it's not my job." You just do it. (Actually, I later learned that excuses don't exist at great organizations of any size.)

When I answered, a woman was crying and asking for help. I took her number, made sure she was all right, and told her we would come and get her. A nurse and I drove eight miles to Milton, Wisconsin, to pick her up and bring her to the treatment center. Three or four days later, when the woman was feeling better after coming out of detoxification, she came up and hugged me. She thanked me for saving her life. I know I didn't save her life. But I did like the hug and the feeling that I made that kind of difference.

As part of my job for the treatment center, I also worked with human resource department leaders in the area and got to know the personnel director at Mercy Hospital in Janesville. So when she offered me a job one day as director of community relations and marketing at the hospital, I took it. I figured that if we did great things at a 35-bed hospital for people with alcohol and drug problems, what must it be like to work in an organization that helps people with cancer, surgeries, and childbirth? I was excited.

Have you ever taken a job and thought you were *competent?*

And then you realized you were *unconsciously incompetent?*

But you don't realize it until you're *consciously incompetent?*

That's when you say, "I don't know what I'm doing!"

Now I know that's a normal way for people to adjust to a job. In fact, it's the reason why it's so critical to provide excellent preceptors and orientation for new staff in health care. Then when their initial excitement fades to an understanding of being consciously incompetent, we can help them through to the next level so they succeed.

I knew I had to learn more about health care. I was like a sponge and read everything I could get my hands on. I did the best I could, and after awhile, I wasn't too bad at it. The CEO liked me and thought I did a good job. As a special ed teacher, I was very focused on tasks so I could help my students maximize their abilities. So at the hospital, whenever the CEO gave me a job, I got it done. After a year and a half I was promoted to Vice President of Planning and Marketing.

I was making more money than I had ever dreamed. People treated me differently—like a big shot. It was a whole new ballgame. That's when I learned how to name-drop. "I'll talk to you later," I'd say. "I gotta go to a department head meeting" or "John, let me get back to you. I have to go see the CEO."

When I became Senior Vice President of Business Development for the system, life was good. The organization was making a lot of money. I learned that was important.

When I went to meetings where there were a lot of other hospital administrators and leaders, I noticed that the conversation immediately steered to talk about financials. As far as I could tell, they didn't talk much about clinical outcomes, patient satisfaction, or employee satisfaction. So I didn't talk about those things either. I wanted to learn their language—feel "a part of" instead of "apart." **So instead of people, we had "FTE's." Our patients were "cost per adjusted discharges." "Market share" was the code word for how many people we were providing services to. When I went to conferences, the key question to ask and answer was always "How's your bottom line?"**

My New Quest

Sometime during this journey, I decided I wanted to be a CEO. At first I didn't think I could ever be a CEO—that I wasn't smart enough. But I was attracted to the idea. I saw some things about that job that I would like for me.

For instance, I noticed that people didn't tell the CEO what to do because he controlled the agenda. I liked that. I grew up in the '60s so I didn't like being told what to do. It appealed to the rebellious side of me that wanted to change things.

I also noticed that our CEO had a parking spot right across from the front door. There was a sign that said, "Reserved for Hospital Administrator." That was attractive to me. I wanted to know why he got to park there right next to the hospital, but I was a little nervous about asking. So when I met an administrative secretary in the cafeteria one day, I said, "I never noticed this myself, but some of the other employees have wondered how come the CEO gets to park right next to the front door of the hospital."

She said, "Oh, well, that's because he comes and goes all day."

I wanted to come and go all day.

I'm a can't-sit-still kind of guy. Plus I wanted to be able to get out on a bad day. If you've ever had a day at work that just sucked, you may have noticed that days that suck, often suck early. They are those five-more-hours-and-I'm-out-of-here kind of days. I thought it would be nice on those days to shoot a quick glance at my watch and say, "Oops, its 11:30. Time for Rotary. Be back in a couple of hours." I also noticed that if the CEO comes in late, it is unlikely that someone is going to stop them and say, "You know, we usually start a couple of hours earlier. Could you be here by 8 a.m.?" The CEO job looked pretty sweet to me.

Of course, I found out that it was a tough job. But I didn't know it at the time. All I knew was that I wanted it. And I knew in order to become a hospital CEO, the organization you work at has to have a good bottom line.

Our system was making money. I thought we were making the money because we were so smart, because we were so vertically integrated, because we had good systems and a good staff. Much of this was true, but, I also found out we had some strategic advantages in Janesville, Wisconsin. First of all, we were the only hospital in a decent-sized town. We also had a great payer mix that was very heavy with commercial payers and just a small percentage of self-pay or Medicaid. This was an important part of the bottom line.

Unfortunately, CEOs of hospitals like that don't often leave to look for a new job. Mercy's CEO wouldn't be leaving anytime soon as far as I could tell. So I told my wife we might have to move so I could find a CEO job.

MOVE TO CHICAGO

When I spoke with a search firm and told them I would like to be a CEO, they asked for a CV and then came back with some bad news. They told me I couldn't be a CEO because I didn't have enough operational experience. They told me I needed to be a Chief Operating Officer (COO) first.

I was hoping I could skip that step. I didn't want to be a COO. I noticed that the COOs stayed all day at the hospital while the CEOs were coming and going from that parking spot.

The search firm also had more bad news for me. They told me I wasn't a high draft pick as a COO, because some people might think location and payer mix had too much to do with our hospital's profitability. "You're going to have to go where we can get you a job," they said. So in January 1993, I ended up on the south side of Chicago in a hospital that had lost nine million dollars in 1992. Although an outside turnaround expert had stopped this hemorrhage, the hospital still had a long way to go.

Yet when I drove down to Holy Cross Hospital in January 1993, I was feeling pretty confident as the new Senior Vice President/COO. I was coming from a very successful financial organization.

But after three months, I discovered things were quite different than they had been back in Wisconsin. They spoke many different languages in Chicago. There were homicides. They had Cocaine-positive babies at the hospital. The hospital had a bad payer mix—mostly government and self-pay. They didn't have leverage with the managed care companies, either. It was hard to keep employees in a city with so many hospitals in the suburbs.

My dream of becoming a CEO wasn't looking so good. Things were bad. Nobody hires a CEO who comes from a COO position at a break-even or money-losing hospital. You've got to be a winner to get out.

I knew I had made a huge career mistake and thought about going back to Mercy in Wisconsin. I figured that maybe I could just sneak back behind my desk. If the CEO acted confused, I could just say, "Oh no, I didn't quit. I was just doing mission work with some poor people in Chicago. I'm back." But I knew that wasn't really the answer.

So I decided to focus on building patient volume first at Holy Cross. But when I began asking physicians to put their patients in our hospital, they told me they were reluctant because of all the complaints about patient care. So I looked at our patient satisfaction rating as reported by an outside company and learned we were in the fifth percentile. When I brought this up, leaders at the hospital told me the tool was bad. The problem was the area we were in. It was the physicians' fault. Only unhappy people filled out the survey.

The CEO told me that he wanted me to focus on patient satisfaction. But I hadn't signed on to do patient satisfaction. I was there to learn how to be a CEO. I thought patient satisfaction was soft stuff and nobody would hire me if I were good at that. I wanted to be busy with managed care negotiations, mergers, consolidations, cash collections, debt financing, re-engineering, hiring physicians, and opening medical centers—things like that.

My only experience with patient satisfaction had been at Mercy in Wisconsin, and it wasn't pretty. Have you ever had a patient complain in your hospital? These people are not quiet. In the middle of the hallway, they yell, *"Where's Administration?"*

Then, like heat-seeking missiles, they come down to Administration and wait for you. After a few of these encounters, I got a beeper and told the secretary to page me if there was a family in the waiting room. Because I wasn't coming back.

The reason I hid was because patient satisfaction seemed like a life sentence. Before the patient complained, I'd never seen that family in my entire life. But after the complaint, they were everywhere. When I went to the grocery store, there they would be in the frozen foods aisle. When I went to the movies, I was afraid to go to the bathroom because they might be in there.

So I always told my assistant to call the nurse manager. Then I would be off the hook. If a family was waiting for me and the nurse manager didn't come in three minutes, she'd get a second call. When she arrived, she'd say those magic words to the family that I longed for: "Why don't we go somewhere else where we can talk?"

The key words were *somewhere else*. Because only then would it be safe to return to my office. So that was my background with patient satisfaction. And now I was in CHARGE of it!

Today, I love patient satisfaction. It represents all the best things about health care. It also led me home to all the things that had once appealed about working in special education and health care in the first place: purpose, worthwhile work, and making a difference.

The executive team at Holy Cross made it a goal to move our patient satisfaction scores from 5th percentile to 75th percentile in a year. But when I called a measurement company to ask for advice, they told me nobody had ever made that kind of a leap in one year.

"So what should I do?" I asked them. They told me it would be key to visit the patient care units. I didn't think that suggestion would be very effective because I had a lot of experience visiting other departments back in Janesville. When I first became a hospital vice president, I had visited the housekeeping department and told them I was the vice president of planning and marketing. They were very nice. I guess I would call it sucking up a little. The security department was also very nice. They knew where my car was parked and took very good care of Administration.

But back in those days, when I went up to my first nursing floor, the second floor orthopedic unit, I didn't get the same kind of reception. When I introduced myself and asked how they were all doing, they really told me. Then they told me some more. The nurses told me about staffing problems, tools and equipment that didn't work, and many more challenges at the hospital that I really didn't want to hear about. So I decided that "managing by walking around" wasn't so helpful.

But at Holy Cross I was desperate to get those numbers up, so I decided to try it anyway. I walked up to a nurse who had a name badge on her upper left shoulder and said, "Hi, Valerie. I'm Quint Studer. I'm the chief operating officer of the hospital. I have been here about six months. I'm in charge of patient satisfaction. Valerie . . . we're *family*."

Have you ever heard that? "We're family?" (Of course, I didn't say we were a *functional* family.) But I went on. "Valerie, you need to focus on patient satisfaction," I explained. "You need to treat people like *you* want to be treated, okay? Like they were your relatives. Oh—and, you need to smile."

How many steps do you think I took with my back to the RNs before one of them made a gagging motion with her finger in her mouth? I will tell you because I have it down to a science. In OB, I could take three steps. In Med Surg, they'll let you take a step and a half. In ICU, they get you on the pivot. And in the ER, they know before you get there. Somebody calls and says, "Guess who's coming?" (with their finger in their mouth).

I went down to my office and waited for the satisfaction scores to go up. Nothing happened. I had no idea what to do next and the problems were mounting.

RETURNING TO PURPOSE

After six months at the hospital, I felt I had made a huge career mistake but didn't want to admit it to myself. So I blamed everything. I blamed labor. I blamed Medicare. I blamed Medicaid. And I blamed Chicago.

After my friend Frank heard me complaining and blaming long enough, he finally said, "You know, Quint, I know what the problem is at Holy Cross Hospital." He handed me an envelope with three decals in it and told me to place one on my mirror at home, one on the mirror of my car, and one on a mirror at work. All three decals said the same thing: *You're looking at the problem.*

He said, "This is about you. You've gotta change."

I didn't like hearing that, but somehow I knew he was right. When he held up the mirror and I looked in it, I knew I needed help. Denial had to go.

In fact, I had heard I was part of the problem before in the early '90s, but I just didn't believe it. I was walking through the hospital at the time when I said to Tim, a housekeeping employee, "This place looks terrible." He looked back at me and said, "The fish starts rotting at the head." I didn't know what he meant then. I thought that was because I didn't do much fishing. Now I know he was speaking about leadership.

But I didn't want any of my colleagues to know I had no idea how to solve the hospital's problems. It might get out that I didn't know what I was doing—which I didn't. So I researched some non-health care companies with reputations for outstanding service. When I learned that Southwest Airlines was setting the standard in customer satisfaction, I went to see them and told them about our patient satisfaction problems.

They asked what I'd been doing to fix it. I said, "I've been going up on the nursing units and telling them to smile." (I think they wanted to gag, too.)

They asked, "Do they have the tools and equipment to do their jobs?"

"I don't know," I said. "I suppose they do."

"Do they have a good supervisor?" they asked me.

"Well, I would think so," I answered.

"Are they feeling rewarded and recognized?" they queried.

"Oh yes," I assured them. "We celebrate Hospital Week."

Then they said, "Quint, this is all about what type of culture you create in the workplace. It's about leadership and employees."

While I listened to their questions, I felt overwhelmed. It became even more clear to me that I really didn't know any of the answers or what to do next.

The folks at Southwest told me to change what I said when I was on the nursing units—that I should say, "We want to make this a better place for you to work. What do I need to do?" They thought the nurses would like that question better. I remember thinking that they didn't have any RNs at Southwest.

I wasn't too excited about going back up there to see the nurses. In fact, I was scared. But I didn't see how I had any choice, because our scores were still low and the clock was ticking. Something had to change. So I did it. When I got there, I saw Valerie, the nurse whom I'd told to smile earlier on. I said, "Valerie, remember me? I am back here to say that we want to make this a better place for you to work. What do I need to do?"

Guess what? She told me. Just like that. I found out that nurses had always wanted what was best for the patient. They were on the right page. I was the one who was lost.

Valerie told me about her copy-machine woes. She said they used to have one on their unit until the hospital took it away and asked two units to share one, which was inconvenient and inefficient for both units. "Whenever we have to make a copy, we have to walk off the unit," she explained. "We miss call lights, and it eats up time we could be spending with patients. Can we please get our copy machine back?"

Southwest was right. She didn't roll her eyes or gag when I asked her *that* question. She just told me what they needed. So I got them a copier. I heard similar things from all the nursing units. Their complaints weren't usually about big stuff. And if I couldn't provide what they requested right away, I explained why.

Once I began asking nursing staff the right questions, things started to improve. In fact, it worked in every department. Turnover decreased and financials improved. We made over one million dollars that year, which is not bad considering the hospital had lost $9 million just a few years earlier. We were trending in the right direction. I began to think that when the CEO assigned me to fixing patient satisfaction, maybe he knew what he was doing after all.

Maybe, I thought, there was light at the end of the tunnel. Maybe I could get out of this hospital now. Or, at the very least, get a new job away from patient satisfaction.

When we hit the 73rd percentile for patient satisfaction in December 1993 (i.e., we were among the top 27 percent of hospitals compared to hospitals nationwide who used the same measurement tool), I felt good. We'd jumped from rock bottom at the 5th percentile and were now just two points away from our lofty goal, six months ahead of schedule.

Then someone passed me a letter that said:

Dear Sister,

My father died at your hospital. It wasn't a matter of if he was going to die, but when. He was in your extended care facility. I'm his only living relative. I was all that he had. My constant worry was that I wouldn't be there when he died. I tried to be at the hospital every moment, but I simply couldn't be there 24 hours a day.

I wasn't there one day and I received a call from a nurse who said, "You need to get here right away." I jumped in my car and got caught in a traffic jam. I pulled up to the hospital and ran inside. As soon as I got to the nursing unit, they told me my father was dead.

But when I went into the room, I saw a nurse there with him. She was sitting down. And holding my father's hand. That nurse told me that my father wasn't alone when he died. She was there. She also told me that my father loved me.

Do you know what a great nurse you have at your hospital?

I found out later that this nurse's shift had already ended when she decided to stay. Knowing the financial challenges we faced at the hospital, the nurse swiped her card and stayed with the patient on her own time. Her values would not let her leave.

At that moment, life changed for me. I felt feelings I had not realized I had lost. I felt the way I had when I was working with special education students and when I drove the woman to the treatment facility and she hugged me and thanked me. I felt a sense of purpose, of doing worthwhile work, and of making a difference.

When I first came to work at that 35-bed Wisconsin hospital, it had been for the right reasons. Somehow along the way, I got lost. But at the moment I read this patient's letter, I wasn't concerned about the 75th percentile. I wanted to make sure patients had a good place where they could come to receive quality care . . . that employees had a good place to work . . . and that physicians had a good place to practice medicine.

That letter changed me. You know why? Because I had been on that unit. I knew those nurses, and I felt part of this difference. I wanted to go find that nurse and thank her. It felt wonderful to have a sense of purpose and worthwhile work again.

We didn't hit 75th percentile that year. We ended up hitting 94th percentile. We even won the Great Comeback of the Year Award for a large hospital, awarded by *Hospitals & Health Networks* and the American Hospital Association. Several months later, our CEO was asked to come speak at a conference on patient satisfaction. He sent me instead since I had championed the effort. I took a couple of other Holy Cross leaders—Liz Jazwiec and Don Dean—and we shared what we had learned.

MOVE TO PENSACOLA

After hearing our story, hospitals started to benchmark Holy Cross. Usually, patient representatives, marketing staff, or a few nurse managers would come to our hospital to learn about what we were doing. In May 1995, some leaders from a Northwest Florida hospital network benchmarked our hospital. In the fall of 1995, they invited me to speak to their leadership team. Then in March 1996, they offered me the administrator position at their flagship hospital. So it turned out patient satisfaction wasn't soft at all. They hired me specifically because I had helped turn it around with solid results at Holy Cross.

So I moved to Florida to become administrator of Baptist Hospital, Inc., which includes: Baptist Hospital, a 492-bed hospital, and Gulf Breeze Hospital, a 60-bed hospital.

While Dick Fulford, administrator of the Gulf Breeze Hospital, reported to me, he didn't need me. He had figured it out long ago. The Gulf Breeze facility ran very well. Dick and his team had done a remarkable job there so I focused my time on the downtown Baptist facility.

I learned a lot of lessons during my journey. While I originally wanted the CEO job back in Wisconsin because of the parking space next to the building, I knew by the time I became president of the hospital that I had to be a good role model. I parked far away—and found I met a lot of staff that way.

When I started, the first thing I did was walk up to employees and say, "Hi, my name is Quint Studer. I'm the new administrator here. I work for you. What should I do today?"

From the way they looked at me I suspected they were thinking, *Maybe a urine screen?* They really wondered about me. But then a nurse said, "Tonight when I leave, it's going to be dark. We work in a pretty tough neighborhood. I park out by the bushes, and those bushes haven't been trimmed for months. I'm worried when I go out to my car that someone could be hiding there. Could you get those bushes trimmed?"

During the next 12 hours, while she was working, we had the bushes trimmed and put up a small fence. When the nurse came out to her car, she noticed and felt safe. We had exceeded her expectations.

By utilizing many of the things I had learned at Holy Cross and other organizations that I studied, our team achieved some remarkable things. In fact, one reason that I took the job was to show that what we had achieved at Holy Cross wasn't due to chance or luck. I wanted to prove that if we hardwired the right behaviors, tools, and techniques and aligned our focus organizationwide, we could get the same great results—even with a different system, different location, and different medical staff.

We did. Patient satisfaction, which ranged between the 9th and the 40th percentiles, soared to the 99th percentile. Our employee turnover dropped from around 30 percent to 12 percent. Our financial performance was rock solid. In fact, Moody's even upgraded our bond rating. In their analysis, they noted that our focus on customer service had shifted market share, making us a more profitable hospital. In addition to adding $1.8 million to our bottom line, Moody's new rating signaled to the investor community that the policy of hospitals putting people first makes good financial sense. Our clinical indicators also registered "excellent." In fact, we lowered our decubitus ulcer rate from 9 percent to 2 percent. And our patient volume soared over 34 percent, a 3.5 market share point movement. We were helping many more people.

We were recognized with numerous awards including the Voluntary Hospital Association Leadership Award (1997), the Modern Healthcare Sodexo Marriott Service Excellence Award (1997), and the Excellence in Risk Management Award by *Modern Healthcare Magazine* (1999). In March 1999, *Inc. Magazine* named me Master of Business. And in 2000, the hospital was awarded the USA Today Quality Cup from *USA Today* and the Rochester Institute of Health.

Today, Baptist is consistently ranked in the top 100 best places to work nationwide by *Fortune Magazine*. Four years after I left, Baptist also won the 2003 Malcolm Baldrige Award. Once the systems and processes are in place to sustain service and operational excellence, an organization is no longer dependent on a particular leader to ensure continued success. I've seen too many good organizations lose good results when a leader leaves. My goal was to hardwire results so that when I left, they would sustain the gains. Hardwiring works.

Through this journey, I learned that results come from hardwiring agendas, evaluations, communication, training, selection, discharge phone calls, thank you notes, and more. This way, the hardwired behaviors drive the system if the leaders change. This is crucial since most staff and physicians will work at a facility longer than the average CEO. Hardwiring excellence supports the organization's values and sustains the gains. This, then, is why I wrote the chapters to come: to lay out the actions and behaviors all organizations can use to hardwire excellence.

BECOMING A FIRE STARTER

During my days at Holy Cross something else was going on. I became a "Fire Starter." Back in 1994, when I spoke at a conference on patient satisfaction, the conference organizers made a tape. It began to be circulated at health care organizations until I was invited to speak at a larger conference in San Francisco.

When I was introduced by a doctor from the Harvard School of Medical Economics, he talked about what we'd achieved at Holy Cross and said, *"Quint's a Fire Starter."*

He went on to explain his use of the term and said that in the earliest civilizations, Fire Starters were people who kept the flame alive. This was important, he said, because if they were successful, the people survived. If they weren't, the people died.

He said, "Today in health care, our flame is low. Employee morale is low. Physician satisfaction is low. The confidence level of patients is low. We need Fire Starters. Quint is a Fire Starter, and he's trying to make the flame brighter."

At the time, I thought he was a little off the deep end. But the more I listened to him, the more I realized I was still hanging around the edges, not wanting to fail. When I got up, I decided I wanted to take the risk. So I said, "I'm Quint Studer, and I want to be a Fire Starter. I want to make a difference." That conference and an article in *Modern Healthcare* about Holy Cross's patient satisfaction originally sparked the interest of organizations to visit Holy Cross. In fact, leaders from 88 organizations came.

When I joined Baptist Hospital, Inc. in Florida, I requested and received release days in my contract to speak to and carry the message to other organizations. We also agreed that I would own the intellectual capital I brought to Baptist and that Baptist would have the right to use it after I left. However, during my first 18 months at Baptist, I didn't speak to groups outside the hospital because I felt I first needed to demonstrate that the success we achieved at Holy Cross could really transfer to another hospital. Eventually, other hospitals started to hear about the results. They started benchmarking—as they had done at Holy Cross—to see what we were doing. Eventually, I began getting requests to speak again, and the number of visitors increased.

As leaders requested specific prescriptive tools and implementation guidelines, I developed a more structured presentation based upon my research and experiences at Holy Cross, Baptist, and other organizations I had visited.

In 1999, I was approached by a marketing company about developing two-day seminars. This provided the impetus for my development of the Nine Principles℠ for service and operational excellence that are described in the following chapters. Since 1999, they have provided an important foundation for hundreds of organizations in creating and sustaining a culture of service and operational excellence.

In the fall of 1999, I found myself at a crossroads. On the one hand, I enjoyed being the president of a hospital and loved working with the employees, physicians, and patients. And in 1999, I was also named executive vice president of the system. I had a great job that I loved with an excellent salary and retirement plan. Results just kept climbing since they were so well hardwired. If I stayed, I could look forward to more years at a rewarding job with a happy retirement in the not-too-distant future. Could I walk away from that kind of security?

On the other hand, I was also increasingly being asked to carry the flame to a wider audience at other health care organizations. I hadn't had a vacation in three years because I had used all my days to carry the message to other hospitals. When I was out speaking, I felt I should be at the hospital. When I was at the hospital, I felt badly about turning down other hospitals. I realized I couldn't do both.

About that time, I read *The Power of Constructive Thinking* by Emmit Fox. He said that sometimes you have to go with your heart and seize the opportunity when a door opens—even if security doesn't seem to be readily apparent. Sometimes people pass over these opportunities, he explained, but if you do the right thing, the right things happen. So I took the leap to help others full-time, left Baptist, Inc., and formed Studer Group, which coaches health care organizations across the country on how to hardwire excellence through the application of prescriptive actions, tools, and techniques.

As Studer Group's partner organizations grew, so did my learning. We were able to capture best practices from Washington, D.C., and Miami to San Diego and New York. We began to develop more prescriptive tools such as rounding logs, discharge phone calls for clinical outcomes, and 30- and 90-day meetings with new employees and share these practices with leaders at our monthly institutes held across the country. We deepened our understanding of what works and why. We were also fortunate to attract coaches from health care organizations nationwide (e.g., physicians, CNOs) who could share their unique expertise from the environments in which they had worked. Today, we represent expertise and cross-fertilization from more than 300 health care organizations nationwide.

I'm very grateful to Parkside Lodge and Mercy Health System in Janesville, Wisconsin, for my early experience in health care; to Holy Cross Hospital in Chicago, Illinois, for helping me find purpose and show that by focusing on employees, physicians, and patients, you can achieve bottomline results; and to Baptist Hospital, Inc. in Pensacola, Florida, for showing how excellence can be hardwired and not dependent upon individual leaders.

What have I learned? I know now that it doesn't matter whether you work in Wisconsin, Illinois, Florida, or California. You can have purpose, do worthwhile work, and make a difference regardless of your geographic location, type of organization, size, patient demographics, payer mix, or other challenges. I also know from experience that any health care organization can go from good to great.

Daily in my travels, I'm reminded how imperative it is for organizations not only to consider their problems, but more importantly, to identify and study the causes of their successes so they can duplicate them. I've also learned that when health care organizations improve their patient, employee, and physician satisfaction, they are rewarded and recognized in dozens of unforeseen and astounding ways. The best recognition is when people feel confident about their care, physicians enjoy practicing medicine, and employees are proud to be part of the organization.

Why do we choose to work in health care? Because it gives us a chance to *make a difference* in the lives of others during our short time on earth. If enough of us do that, we will make this world a better place for our children and grandchildren.

So today I coach for Studer Group. And I'm still a Fire Starter on an incredible journey. Every day, I am in awe of the passion, creativity, and commitment of the many Fire Starters I meet who are inspired and determined to make health care better for patients, employees, and physicians across this great nation. There are thousands of us now. And this relights my flame every day.

- Prescriptive To Do's

Principles

Pillar Results

- Results Tied to Each Pillar

Purpose Worthwhile Work and Making a Difference

Passion

- Self-Motivation

HARDWIRING
EXCELLENCE

Chapter Two

@

Healthcare Flywheel

Throughout my travels, I have found that most health care organizations are good. In fact, about 85 percent of patients in the average hospital rank care as good or very good (or say they are satisfied or very satisfied with their care). However, sometimes that is exactly the problem. Feeling "good enough" is often the biggest barrier for an organization in moving to the next level. There may be no sense of urgency.

The challenge, then, is how to move from good to great (and great to greater) so we can sustain the gains' and take our success to another level. Sometimes when I ask hospital CEOs how their RN turnover is, they'll say, "Not bad. We're within the state average." I think that in health care, at times, we work at the middle. But we can't afford to do that. We must aim to be the very best.

Since the inception of Studer Group, we've been fortunate to help guide this journey at some of the very finest organizations in the world. They are truly leaders in their field. Yet, they want to get even better. Increasingly, I notice that it is most often the leaders at great organizations who are most committed to further improvement.

Those who succeed do so because their commitment flows from the right reasons: They want to provide better care for patients, a better workplace for employees, and a better place to practice medicine for physicians.

It all starts with a commitment to **Purpose, Worthwhile Work and Making a Difference.** These are the values that rest at the core of the journey and at the hub of the Healthcare Flywheel[SM]. I've met many, many health care professionals, and nearly all of them say they are driven by these core values. This is why most of us went to work in health care in the first place—and likely the reason why you are reading this book. (See? The good always want to get better.)

HEALTHCARE FLYWHEEL[SM]

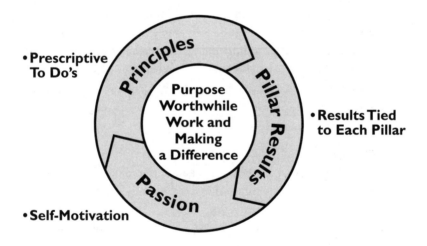

• **Prescriptive To Do's**

Principles

Pillar Results

Purpose Worthwhile Work and Making a Difference

• **Results Tied to Each Pillar**

Passion

• **Self-Motivation**

The Healthcare Flywheel shows how organizations can create momentum for change by engaging the passion of their employees to apply prescriptive actions guided by Nine Principles[SM] of service and operational excellence to achieve bottom-line results. By continually reinforcing how daily choices and actions connect back to these core values at the hub of the Flywheel (purpose, worthwhile work, and making a difference), leaders will reinforce these behaviors and effect change more quickly.

SELF-MOTIVATION

The Flywheel is initially turned by passion. Fortunately, people in health care are passionate and self-motivated. Who but a self-motivated person could hold a dying infant in her arms or witness the death of a patient he has come to care about and still come to work every day for more of the same? Of course, the job description also requires many to work with complex reimbursement, keep current on an ever-expanding array of medications and changing procedures in a 365 day-24/7 work environment. The problem is not motivation. It is the ways in which we unintentionally de-motivate employees.

Imagine, for example, that your boss called you into his or her office. Would your first thought be *Here comes more reward and recognition?*

Let's say you work in facility engineering and the telephone rings. You answer, "Facility engineering. This is Debra. How can I help you?"

And someone says, "Yes, this is the staff in the OR. We were just talking today and wanted to call and let you know the temperature is good. It's very comfortable. Thank you."

Does this happen often in your department?

See . . . in health care we are trained to notice the problem, hone in on the negative variance, react to failing systems, disease, and illness. We are professionally trained to be problem-spotters. To a point, this is a good way to avoid mechanical failures, improve financial operations, and ensure quality clinical care. Unfortunately, noticing the negative does not provide the foundation for a positive work culture. I learned that to create a positive relationship, it takes three positive comments to balance every negative one. I am not suggesting that we stop noticing what's wrong; the goal is to substantially increase our awareness and celebration of all that is right. Indeed, there is much to celebrate in health care today. In chapter 5, I will share prescriptive tools you can use to shift your focus organizationwide to what's working well. This is a critical step in creating the kind of organizational culture that turns the flywheel. Without it, there will be little movement and it will not be possible to sustain the gains that are made.

So in summary, we are fortunate to work with so many who have passion for what they do. But it's important that we don't unwittingly sap this innate self-motivation. Once we successfully engage employees on our quest for excellence, the Flywheel begins to spin.

PRESCRIPTIVE TO DO'S

These are the techniques, tools, and behaviors that will achieve results under goals that organizations set under Five Pillars of Excellence: People, Service, Quality, Finance, and Growth (see chapter 3). The prescriptive To Do's will be described throughout the following chapters on the Nine Principles of service and operational excellence. I developed these guiding principles to help leaders focus on how to implement actions that will have the greatest impact. They provide a step-by-step road map to getting and sustaining results.

For example, if a leader is discouraged because of high employee turnover, high nursing agency costs, or scheduling challenges, a motivational talk will only serve as a band-aid for the real problem. Instead, I recommend training a leader how to reduce turnover. This will improve morale and get results as described below.

WHAT ARE RESULTS?

When the prescriptive To Do's are implemented, leaders:

- lower staff turnover;

- raise employee, physician, and patient satisfaction;

- improve service and quality;

- create greater capacity to serve more patients; and

- ensure a healthier bottom line for their organizations.

As employees see the results of their initial efforts, the Flywheel turns faster and momentum builds. This passion fuels more results in a success spiral. Progress toward goals is measured under metrics established under the Five Pillars previously mentioned (People, Service, Quality, Finance, and Growth).

Many leaders ask me, "How can I keep my staff motivated?" I urge them to focus on two things: (1) drive the prescriptive To Do's that are included throughout this book because they bring results, and (2) always connect results back to purpose, worthwhile work, and making a difference. That feeds and strengthens self-motivation.

I find that the most successful leaders understand and organize around Passion, Prescription, and Results because this combination leads all individuals back to the hub of our deep and universal yearning to have purpose, do worthwhile work, and make a difference. In fact, I urge leaders to always connect the actions they ask of their employees back to how they make a difference and serve an important purpose. They need to hear this.

WHAT HAPPENED TO OUR PRIORITIES IN HEALTH CARE?

In 1998, the American Hospital Administration (AHA) asked hospital CEOs what was on their "To Do" list to move their organizations forward. They received 3,700 responses from leaders who ranked their priorities:

1: Upgrading Technology/Information Systems

2: Integrating Delivery System/Forming a Provider Network

3: Developing New Services/Diversifying into Different Business Lines

4: Re-engineering Business Processes

5: Recruiting Physicians

6: Re-engineering Clinical Services

7: Forming a Physician Hospital Organization

8: Controlling Costs

9: Developing a Medical Services Organization

10: Merging/Consolidating

11: Building/Expanding/Renovating

Source: *AHA News,* March 9, 1998. American Hospital Association Leadership Monitor Survey by the HSM Group.

Employees, patients, and physicians never made the CEOs' top ten list.

In fact, when *Modern Healthcare Magazine* reported on the study in a May 11, 1998 article, it said that the study found that executives were not walking the talk: "The report concluded that while health care executives say *customer satisfaction* and *employee retention* are the most important aspects of their business, they fail to invest adequately in either."

I believe these leaders have strong core values and are committed to long-term success. It's just so easy to lose focus when we are putting out fires at every turn. I was certainly guilty of that for many years. For instance, training budgets were hard to come by in those days (and still are today). But consistent, quality training and preceptorship are not disposable budget items. As we face historic workforce shortages and so many other obstacles, I believe that well-trained staff and skilled leadership are non-negotiable.

I think that the results of AHA's survey were predictive of the challenges we face today. Fast forward to the American College of Healthcare Executives' October 2003 survey, where 58 percent of responding CEOs said personnel shortages were one of their top three concerns. Workforce shortages have required employees and physicians to become a priority for now. But it can't be another quick fix. Employees, physicians, and patients must always be at the top of the organization's To Do list because they drive everything else. That's how we hardwire excellence for the long term.

I know that all leaders want to create the right environment for patients, staff, and physicians. It's just that we get distracted and lost as we are bombarded by new crises. But when we get uncomfortable, our values call us back home. Today, many leaders are being called back home. If you are reading this book, welcome home. If the leaders of your organization purchased this book for you, then you are indeed fortunate to work for an organization committed to purpose, worthwhile work, and making a difference.

It's Still About the Patient

Note from a Nurse Who Attended "Taking You and Your Organization to the Next Level"

> Attending mandatory conferences ranks high on my list of Least Favorite Things to Do. How can "they" ask me to do any more than I already do? I asked myself. There's no time in my schedule. I can think of a million other excuses, but I don't have the time for that either!
>
> So I attended out of obedience, but with a reluctant heart and closed mind. I'm an old nurse. (I could say I am "seasoned" or "experienced," but I just feel old.) I was quite sure I would not learn anything new about how to care for my patients. The thing about us "old" nurses,

though, is that as we age, we forget things. But can we forget the basic and fundamental things? I had.

For me, this Institute was like a stick of dynamite. It blew a hole in the concrete wall of resistance that I had so carefully constructed between change and me. What took years to build was blown apart in minutes. What I thought was a masterpiece was now rubble. Then, there beneath the rubble, I got a glimpse of myself 30 years ago as a wide-eyed new graduate ready to take on the world with my whole career ahead of me.

It was painful to realize how I had forgotten the vows I made as a nurse. When had my heart grown cold and hard? That dynamite explosion could have been fatal. But I didn't die. Instead it felt more like having surgery. My closed mind was opened! My heart of stone was replaced with a heart of flesh! My failing vision is now clearer than it's been in years! And you know what? It's not about me! It has always been and is still about the patient!

Thank you for rekindling the fire of passion and compassion within the heart of this nurse!

Most sincerely,

Susan, RN

FLYWHEEL MOVING BACKWARDS

When I was hired at Baptist Hospital, Inc. in Pensacola, Florida, the flywheel wasn't moving the way people wanted it to. In February 1996, an employee attitude survey had showed that they were deeply unhappy. In fact, the measurement company said they were some of the most unhappy employees they had ever tested.

At most organizations, employees tend to be less satisfied with compensation and benefits and more satisfied in categories such as, "I like my work" and "I like my department." But at Baptist, employees rated their satisfaction very low in 15 out of 18 categories measured.

The scariest thing about that survey was the disparity of results between top managers and supervisors. Supervisors were ranked below average. But Administration was even worse.

Supervisors could say, "Whew! We were rated a negative two, but top management got a negative eight. I'm surprised we were even able to get a negative two since we were dragging them around!"

At Studer Group, we find this isn't unusual in employee satisfaction surveys at many health care organizations, but it is dangerous because it creates a barrier to creating a culture of true teamwork. To me, this signifies a critical need to consistently invest in leadership and management training so employees can have faith in and align their behaviors with those who guide their organizations.

It also isn't unusual to hear of low survey response rates to employee satisfaction surveys either. Only 39 percent of employees bothered to complete the survey at Baptist. It's easy to rationalize that we only hear from the complainers—or that the survey was poorly timed because (insert excuse: "there was a merger then," "it was a busy time of year," etc.). Of course this disappointing data caused pain. No leader wants to have a workplace that isn't good. But at times, denial can be so great that rationalization and excuses just kick in. But I believe employees work very hard to ensure their feedback is accurate. By listening, we can learn about opportunities to become better.

While a number of things may have influenced Baptist's February 1996 survey results, they were really a blessing because they provided a sense of urgency and a platform for change. They were the foundation upon which we worked to build a culture of service and operational excellence.

It Doesn't Have to be this Way

One of the biggest challenges I find in health care is the "we/they" attitude between middle management and administration. This attitude is pervasive with respect to talk about satisfaction surveys, budgets, or salaries.

I was a *we/they* leader. I was a department manager, and I learned how to deliver bad news with the best of them.

"Bob," I'd say, "I went to HR about your pay raise, but they said no," or, "I fought for us on the budget. Here's the best I could do."

Who's the bad guy? Not me. It's Administration—top management. I positioned administration negatively for my own comfort. I didn't do it on purpose. I did it because no one trained me *not* to. As one leader said to me recently at the end of my two-day talk, "It was just so natural that I was unconscious I was even doing it."

Now, what are the chances that any leader is going to get everything he requested in the budget? What are the odds that she is going to come back after the meeting and say to staff, "Unbelievable! We didn't ask for enough! Yep, he thinks we're understaffed."

You just don't hear things like that. I have also seen senior leaders make these excuses . . .

"If I could, I would, but the Board is leaning **heavy** on me on this one."

or . . .

"I'm open to it, but Corporate says no."

When we blame others, we take purpose out of the equation for the employee. Employees want to be aligned with leaders. They want to work beside and for leaders with the right purpose and intent. When attendees leave Studer Group's two-day Institute, I ask them to list actions they will take as a result of having attended. The number-one behavior they resolve to change is to "stop blaming administration." Creating and sustaining a culture of excellence is all about the willingness to take individual ownership of problems and opportunities.

This holds true for senior leaders as well. At the very best organizations, the leadership team is completely aligned with respect to objectives, work, and evaluation.

THE HEALTHCARE FLYWHEEL REQUIRES CHANGE

Change, especially in health care, is never easy. What we're talking about involves making adjustments. While changing clinical procedures is easy and familiar, changing leadership techniques is often more difficult and not within our comfort zones. There are many barriers to change, including:

Denial. I was willing to look at labor, Medicare, or Medicaid, but I wasn't willing to look at me.

Rationalization. It's easy to come up with excuses. Pointing to staffing challenges is a favorite.

At Baptist Hospital, Inc. in Pensacola, I was told our high employee turnover was due to the fact that we were a military town. Two years later, when turnover was down substantially, I noticed that we were still a military town. As long as we could blame the military, we didn't try to fix it. Because it wasn't our fault. What could we do? Once we agreed to do away with the rationalization, we were able to look at specific ways to improve employee selection, orientation, and training to ensure the individuals we hired would be successful. We focused on improving employee satisfaction to increase retention. Rationalization is a barrier to solutions.

Blame. At Holy Cross Hospital in Chicago, we blamed the homeless. They'd sit in our ER. And once they were treated, we discharged them back into the cold. Therefore, we explained, they were giving us a low score on patient satisfaction because they probably weren't happy about that.

Then one day, somebody asked, "We send the survey to people's homes, right?"

"Yep."

"Then, how do the homeless get it?"

It's so easy to assign blame.

Uniqueness. Every health care organization is unique in its obstacles and opportunities. Unfortunately, that makes it easy to discount survey satisfaction scores that compare us to peer organizations or organizations nationwide. "We can't be compared because we're different," we say. I call this tendency to explain away our mediocre results "terminal uniqueness." Organization size and location are two of the most common excuses here.

Unwillingness. When I first arrived at Baptist Hospital, I was walking through an administrative work area one day when I met an employee who treated me terribly. Even the other employees were embarrassed. When I got back to Administration, I said, "I just met the *rudest* woman!"

They said, "Oh, you met Mary."

I asked, "Doesn't her behavior and attitude impact other employees?"

They said, "Oh no. They just ignore her."

The problem is that what gets tolerated gets accepted. Let me explain. In order to move your organization to the next level, not everybody will get to make the trip.

A hospital is not a rehabilitation center for wayward staff. Perhaps you're afraid that if you start firing those people, you'll be understaffed. I want to assure you that this won't be the case.

The word gets out in departments where low performers and employees with bad attitudes are held accountable. More people want to work there and those that do have higher morale.

One time a nurse leader came up to me and said, "Quint, I have a real problem. My unit is short-staffed. Nobody wants to work there. The work is tough because it's non-stop and we work like crazy. I can't get people to work on my unit. What should I be doing?"

I told her the first thing she should do is stop telling everyone how bad it was to work in her area. "You and your staff are running all over the hospital saying what a terrible place this is to work," I explained. "What nurse wants to go there? It is a self-fulfilling prophecy!" I suggested this nurse leader sit down with her staff and ask, "What do we need to do so this is a good place to work for all of us?" Then I told her to make sure she did it. Use the concept of the mirror decals I described earlier.

In health care, when one bad thing creates another, we call it a death spiral. When you create a great place for staff to work, vacancies will decrease, morale will rise, and the resulting ownership behaviors will translate to better service, quality, financials, and growth. This is a success spiral.

Not Skilled. I believe individuals want to be effective leaders. But they need training. Maybe they don't know how to do it or what to ask for. Maybe they've asked, but have been told no so often that they've stopped asking. Organizations that invest in training live their values by giving employees the skills they need to be successful. In working with hundreds of hospitals, I have found that most organizations don't spend enough time on skill development for leaders. There are no quick fixes. The key is to build the right competencies into each leader so they can be successful. This is a value dividend.

If we allowed an untrained clinician to care for a patient, it would be considered medical malpractice. Since an engaged, aligned workforce is so critical to hardwiring excellence, I believe that not investing in leadership development is the equivalent of organizational malpractice.

In fact, we have found that approximately 39 percent of employees who leave a job do so due to their relationship with their supervisor. We owe it to the patients, families, physicians, and our employees to train leaders. We owe it to the leaders, too.

HI, I WISH I NEVER MET YOU

E-mail sent to Quint Studer after attending Taking You and Your Organization to the Next Level

> Well, I attended your program in June because my patient satisfaction team asked me to attend. I really didn't want to go. I have a fear of flying anyway. Plus, I really don't like customer service training programs.
>
> So I'm sitting in your workshop when I realize that "I'm the man in the mirror." I thought, Wow, let's try it. So I scripted myself, and what do you know? I started having meaningful conversations with staff. I found out what they needed, and got them the tools and equipment to do their jobs. What a difference this is making for me. I have a new-found purpose (and so have the people who work for me).
>
> And yes, I experienced everything you said I would: the push backs, the barriers are all there. I'm dealing with them, but the first one was me. At first I told my Admin team that we should take our time thinking about when and how to implement all this. But now I'm having so much success that I understand the fundamental need to "just do it." Scripting ... hardwiring ... thank you notes ... outcomes orientation. I'm driving everyone crazy. It's really a lot of fun exceeding your patients' expectations. You really connected with me at the CEO level in your talk. Every CEO needs this wake-up call. I finally realized I was not

skilled at talking to my employees until I learned from you how to do it.

Thanks,
Paul
Hospital CEO

UNDERSTANDING SOMETIMES FOLLOWS ACTION

In working with many organizations, experience has shown us that one of the most difficult concepts for leaders to accept is that a person might not understand a behavior until *after* they do it. For example, I got a note recently from a nurse leader who said that she'd been rounding for outcomes (a practice we teach) for a while. She characterized the positive results from rounding as "unbelievable." And yet, she said, it was only after she did it, and did it for a while, that she understood. She had to perform the behavior before she could experience the results.

Understanding comes last.

Until a person can see the result from doing a prescribed behavior, it won't make complete sense.

It's all about action. And it must begin with a decision to act.

A man named Ed once asked me, "If there are two frogs on a lily pad and one decides to jump off, how many do you have left?" "One," I answered, anxious to get back to work. But Ed said there were two.

At first, I was concerned about Ed's mathematical abilities, but then he explained. Making a decision and taking action are two separate behaviors. Some people will decide to jump but never do it. Others will act.

For a long time, I was in the former category. I would make decisions and commend myself for making them (like deciding to go on a diet!), but not act. Or not take enough sustained action. I would say that I was going to hold people more accountable, but not actually do it. The following chapters describe recommended actions that have achieved results at hundreds of organizations. I am confident they will work at your organization too. But only if you actually act and continue to act.

You Can Always Get Better

As I've said, it's usually the good who want to get better. When I first met Bill, he was an excellent 30-year CEO at a great Arkansas hospital (now retired). He came with his leadership team to Pensacola, Florida, to learn about our success.

At the end of the day, I expressed my admiration for his continued commitment to becoming a better leader. In fact, I said, "Bill, you're a much better CEO than me and you've been doing this for over 30 years. What could you take away from a day like this?"

He looked at me and said, *"Spotlight the performers.* I've always had the tendency to shy away from that because I didn't want to hurt anyone's feelings. But when I get back, I'm going to spotlight the performers."

When Bill went back, that's what he did. Since he had one nursing unit that consistently scored high in patient satisfaction, he invited them to a meeting of department managers and directors and explained to all what a great job they had done. He told everyone that when he was out in the community and people told him that their family members had been on that unit, he always felt relaxed because he knew they had received great care.

Within six months, Bill had *all* of his nurse leaders up front at the department head meeting. His action had incentivized every unit to work harder to meet the recognized standard of excellence. I have found that it is important to spotlight the performers, even when it makes others uncomfortable initially.

We have to get comfortable with discomfort because we will experience it frequently when we seek to change the status quo. That's why strong leadership requires so much courage.

When that Arkansas hospital's patient satisfaction skyrocketed through the roof, it was my pleasure to travel there and present Bill with one of Studer Group's first Fire Starter awards. The room was packed with employees. And Bill, who was a recognized leader in health care with many, many national and state awards to his credit—cried as he accepted that plaque from me. His staff honored him with a standing ovation.

There's something wonderful about doing the right thing for patients and employees. There's also something special about having your employees recognize and appreciate what you've been up to.

You may already work for one of the best organizations in the nation. Or perhaps you are one of the leading professionals in your field. If you are, I suspect you want to get even better. It comes with the territory.

Bill taught me to always be out in the field learning. And to always strive for ways to get better. To look for new tools and techniques to turn the Flywheel faster.

When a hospital creates passion and uses the prescriptive To Do's that are guided by the Nine Principles I will outline, the Flywheel begins to turn with ever-increasing results. As employees increasingly feel a sense of purpose and understand how their behaviors and actions make a difference, anything begins to seem possible. The sky's the limit!

Patients receive better care. Employees take pride in working for such an excellent organization, and they line up to work there. Physicians refer more patients. Revenues increase. Leaders are more equipped to lead. Training is recognized as essential.

And the Flywheel spins.

On the Power of Passion

Excerpted from March 1999 INC. Magazine *"90-Day Check Up"*
Interview with Quint

Inc.: What sort of rewards and recognition [do you use]?

Quint Studer: Every company has outstanding people. We make heroes of them. One of our nurses, Cyd Cadena, called up a lady who had been hospitalized to see how she was doing at home. She was in a wheelchair, and she was depressed because she didn't have a wheelchair ramp. The family was so busy working on home health care and a whole bunch of other things that they didn't get a chance to put in a ramp. Well, Cyd called our plant-management person, Don Swartz. And guess what Don did? He built a ramp. Don didn't ask, "Can I do it?" I found out about it because the patient called me. Now we tell that story all over the whole organization. What did we tell our people it was OK to do? Break a few rules. Take a few risks. Don is a star. You have to celebrate your legends.

CHAPTER THREE

PRINCIPLE 1
COMMIT TO EXCELLENCE

The journey to becoming a world-class organization begins with a firm and measurable commitment to excellence (Principle 1). What defines "excellence"? Excellence is when employees feel valued, physicians feel their patients are getting great care, and patients feel the service and quality they receive are extraordinary. A commitment to excellence positively impacts the bottom line while also allowing an organization to live out its mission and values. It aligns staff and leaders and puts the "why" back into health care.

RUNNING A GREAT HOSPITAL

Committing to excellence also means much more than just improving service. It's about excellence across the board. That's why there are Five Pillars instead of just one.

When I was senior vice president of Holy Cross Hospital (Chicago, Ill.) and then president of Baptist Hospital, Inc. (Pensacola, Fla.), I was just as pleased with our improved clinical outcomes and financial performance as I was with lower employee turnover and the higher volume of people coming to our hospital. It was no coincidence that these things occurred around the same time. Results in People, Service, Quality, Finance, and Growth are interrelated.

I have noticed that in health care, there seems to be a new "program" or "flavor of the month" initiative every two years or so that requires us to shift our focus to address the latest threat or newest crisis. During my 20-year career in health care, I lived through vertical integration, horizontal integration, service lines, product lines, physician strategies, re-engineering, utilization management, and a focus on the revenue cycle.

Since the environment is constantly changing, the question becomes, "How can we create a culture that can adjust and respond to change?" I believe the answer is to hardwire excellence.

When I held my first employee forum at Baptist, I showed the Five Pillars to the staff and emphasized organizational goals and results. Someone asked me, "What do we call this new program?" I told them it was called "Running a Great Hospital." I am tired of programs—and I think the physicians and staff are, too.

In 1999, I made a number of presentations for *Inc. Magazine* on how to create the right work culture. As a result, an examiner for the Malcolm Baldrige National Quality Award contacted me to share how the Nine Principles were aligned with the Baldrige criteria. I have found that the Nine Principles attain results, and those results often lead to awards. I congratulate those who receive them. I also congratulate the many excellent organizations who may never apply for such awards but whose achievements in creating and sustaining excellence are widely recognized by employees, physicians, and patients.

In my opinion though, the best award an organization can really win is the confidence of their community . . . when an employee goes home and says to their family, "I work in a great place." And a physician tells a colleague, "That hospital is a really wonderful place to practice medicine." And patients and their families say how good they feel about the care they are receiving. The success of the organization as a whole often becomes so evident to everyone—both inside and outside of the hospital—that the role of senior leaders is virtually transparent.

I think Lao-Tzu says it best: *"An expert craftsman leaves no mark."*

For me, the light bulb first went on when the American Hospital Association's *Hospitals & Health Networks* named Holy Cross Hospital (HCH) the winner of its Great Comeback Award for large hospitals. Our CEO Mark Clement suggested sending staff—in place of senior leaders—to accept the award.

And he was right. If we truly credit our staff with making the difference, shouldn't they be the ones accepting awards and getting their photos in the newspaper instead of top executives? When a group of HCH's employees accepted that award, one CEO asked where the senior leaders were and how HCH had accomplished what it had. One of the representatives from Plant Ops was able to share specifically what his department had done and also explain what the hospital had accomplished in great detail. When he had finished, there was no doubt that he was an excellent representative of our organization.

When success comes, I think the credit should go to staff, physicians, and volunteers. Because while leaders come and go, the key to sustaining a culture of excellence is the commitment by an organization's Board of Directors, employees, and physicians. As a leader, the goal is to hardwire excellence so that sustaining it is not dependent on one or a small group of individuals.

In the late 1990s when I was President at Baptist, I once handed out a fictional newspaper story to all staff at an Employee Forum. I told them that, while surfing the Internet, I must have hit a "hot key" that blasted me electronically into the future or something . . . because I landed on the *New York Times* Web site where I read a front-page article titled "Expert

Craftsmen Leave No Mark." The article talked about health care 20 years from now. It said that health care had never been better. Patients were confident in their caregivers, physicians were very satisfied in the practice of medicine, and people were lining up to work in health care. Then it went on to explain how this movement began when a group of leaders and employees had a vision to make health care a better place for patients to receive care, physicians to practice medicine, and employees to work. Why, the author wondered, was it so difficult to trace the origin of this great revolution? And at the end of the article, the author surmised that expert craftsmen leave no mark.

I've since given this letter to leaders at many organizations to use as a tool for cultural change in their own organizations as they seek to follow that same credo.

Today, our employees are well-versed in the practice of hardwiring excellence. Some coaches have worked in previous positions as leaders in organizations that have been quite successful on this journey. And many coaches still work for these organizations.

Organizations we work with have won awards that range from best employer in their community to making the list of the top 100 hospitals in the U.S. They have received state quality awards and magnet status in nursing, are named as best employers by *Fortune Magazine*, and have won the Malcolm Baldrige Award.

While leaders often call to say thank you, we always pass it back. The credit belongs to the implementer.

How to Align an Organization into Operational Pillars

The Five Pillars provide the foundation for setting organizational goals and direction for service and operational excellence. They also provide the consistency and focus over time that allow an organization to resist new fad programs.

We find that the Pillar model helps organizations to understand both their goals and their current position with respect to those goals on a system-wide basis. It's not a completely new concept. In his wonderful book *Creating the New American Hospital: A Time for Greatness* (John Wiley & Sons, 1993) author Clay Sherman expressed the concept of four Pillars very well. I adapted his model by adding a fifth Pillar (which I define as Growth, or access) and moving "cost" within a new Finance Pillar, which better describes financial goals for me.

Together, the Five Pillars also provide the framework for an evaluation process, since all leaders are evaluated against established metrics under each Pillar. (See chapter 9 for more information on the leader evaluation tool.) In addition, the Five Pillars help keep the organization balanced in its short- and long-term objectives. This Five Pillar foundation for excellence is not the program of the month or the buzzword of the year. It sticks. So I am grateful to Clay Sherman for his Pillar model and his influence. He has been a Fire Starter in my life.

The Nine Principles provide a road map to achieving goals under these Five Pillars. It's a step-by-step process—similar to a clinical pathway—that takes you from where you are to where you want to be. Often after learning about these principles, people say to me, "But Quint, this is just common sense!" "Yes," I answer, "but uncommonly practiced."

Principle 1, *Commit to Excellence*, means setting measurable goals—or desired results—under each of the Five Pillars. Organizations soon see how almost every aspect of what they do is interrelated and has a cause-and-effect relationship in other areas. For example, you can't talk about service (the Service Pillar) without discussing people, quality, finance, or growth. It's very difficult to achieve high patient satisfaction with high employee turnover. CNOs nationwide will confirm that once nursing turnover goes down, so will agency costs, and patients will be moved through the hospital more efficiently to reduce medically unnecessary days and increase capacity. Physicians will refer more of their patients to the hospital because they appreciate the value of standardization and repetition and fewer delays that a retained staff will provide for them. As a result, you will increase your organization's capacity to help more people.

While some organizations choose to add a sixth Pillar (community), I will focus on the core Five Pillars in the chapters to come: Service, Quality, People, Finance, and Growth. Once the organization has aligned its goals, work plan, and evaluation to the Five Pillars, everyone will work together to achieve them.

To hardwire the strategic direction of the organization, I recommend three things:

- Set all meeting agendas by Pillar to provide focus.

- Establish a Leader Evaluation tool by Pillar to create accountability.

- Create department communication boards by Pillars to update staff on measurable progress.

In fact, you can do the first action today. (Stop here and print out the "Meeting Agenda by Pillar" template at *www.studergroup.com.*)

SAMPLE GOALS

What do goals look like under the Five Pillars? Here is an example of first-generation early start-up goals:

Service

- Achieve average percentile ranking of patient satisfaction on hospital survey greater than 95th percentile.

- Reduce claims by 25%.

(Note: As the organization matures, the goals mature. For instance early on, patient satisfaction goals are useful under the

Service Pillar. But eventually, that goal should transition to measures that result from higher patient satisfaction, such as reduced claims, lower legal fees, and reduced malpractice expense.)

BOTTOM LINE RESULTS

SERVICE	QUALITY	PEOPLE	FINANCE	GROWTH
REDUCED CLAIMS	IMPROVED CLINICAL OUTCOMES	REDUCED TURNOVER	IMPROVED OPERATING INCOME	HIGHER VOLUME
REDUCED LEGAL EXPENSES	DECREASED NOSOCOMIAL INFECTIONS	REDUCED VACANCIES	DECREASED COST PER ADJUSTED DISCHARGE	INCREASED CAPITAL
REDUCED MALPRACTICE EXPENSE	REDUCED LENGTH OF STAY	REDUCED AGENCY COSTS	IMPROVED COLLECTIONS	INCREASED REVENUE
	REDUCED RE-ADMITS	REDUCED PRN	REDUCED ACCOUNTS RECEIVABLE	DECREASED LEFT WITHOUT TREATMENT IN THE ED
	REDUCED MEDICATION ERRORS	REDUCED OVERTIME	REDUCED ADVERTISING COSTS	REDUCED OUTPATIENT NO-SHOWS
		REDUCED PHYSICALS AND COST TO ORIENT	IMPROVED STAFF PRODUCTIVITY	INCREASED PHYSICIAN ACTIVITY

Other sample goals under each of the Five Pillars and their economic linkages.

People

- Reduce average employee turnover rate to 17% or less overall, with RN turnover at 11% or lower.

Quality

- Reduce incidence of hospital acquired skin-pressure ulcers to 3% or less.

Finance

- Increase annual operating income margin to 4% or greater.

Growth

- Increase total outpatient visits 9% or greater over previous year.

- Increase total admissions 5%.

When Studer Group works with hospitals directly, we begin the goal-setting process by working with a hospital's senior leadership team and suggest they limit the number of goals to a maximum of ten across all Five Pillars.

SYNERGY OF THE PILLARS

One of the best things about aligning goals under the Five Pillars is the way they achieve results together. For example, preventing pressure ulcers is an important goal to set under the Quality Pillar. According to the Health Care Advisory Board, health care-acquired nosocomial infections can cost between $10,000 and $20,000, depending on the type and severity of the infection, with the cost of health care-acquired decubitus ulcers estimated at $28,681. I know that at Baptist pressure ulcers cost us $23,000 each. And typically, five percent of patients will acquire pressure ulcers during an inpatient stay. So better prevention will result in substantial cost reduction under the Finance Pillar. One way we can achieve this is to better support our employees by recognizing and rewarding their prevention efforts (Service). When barriers are removed to provide quality care and employees see how their efforts make a difference, employee satisfaction rises and turnover drops (People). Since improved quality outcomes increase physician satisfaction, they refer more patients and create greater volume (Growth) and higher revenues (Finance) for the hospital.

Having worked with many organizations, I find it interesting that the Service Pillar is often the last to see results (i.e., patient satisfaction). Organizations typically see movement toward goals in the People Pillar first because it is easier to increase employee retention. Patients, however, may be touched by nearly 60 employees during an inpatient stay. So, while a one-on-one conversation with an employee may have a great impact on retention, it will require a total organizational effort to move patient satisfaction results significantly.

The next Pillar where organizations typically see results is Quality. Once the organization enjoys high employee retention, clinical indicators begin to improve. This is because a retained staff is more effective and efficient. They are well-trained; invested in the success of the organization; and working effectively as a team.

When an organization commits to excellence, it creates a culture where employees want to work. In fact, as health care faces epic workforce shortages, I believe that a core focus on employee retention (rather than recruitment) will serve organizations best. Hospitals will ensure that they keep their top performers and also attract the very best new job candidates. Recently, in fact, I received a note from a hospital CEO who was elated that they had just hired the top nursing graduate in her class. She said that she'd trained in several hospitals, but the culture of this hospital was phenomenal. It was a team she wanted to belong to.

After Quality, Growth is the next Pillar to move. In fact, all it takes is one great department, like a one-day surgery center, for example, to get started. In a one-day surgery center, patients will come in contact with a smaller subset of physicians and employees. Their impression will not be affected by all the employees who provide services (e.g., more clinicians, food service, housekeeping) during a three- or four-day inpatient stay.

As organizations experience gains in the People, Service, Quality, and Growth Pillars, the Finance Pillar reaps the rewards all along the way. From reduced claims and lower agency costs, to lower length of stay and improved access, hospitals will see these gains transfer directly to the bottom line.

The last Pillar to get results is usually Service.

The results in the Service Pillar do come. When organizations implement leader rounding, the use of key words, and other prescriptive actions as outlined in this book, the patient and family's perception of service increases . . . as demonstrated by higher patient and physician satisfaction. And high patient satisfaction will ultimately lead to fewer claims and lower malpractice costs. In essence, every Pillar creates bottom line results.

In fact, once a hospital has set goals under the Pillars, we can predict exactly what their return on investment will be when they meet the benchmarks they have set. One organization, for example, found it could add $2.1 million to the bottom line for each percentage point it reduced employee turnover.

We recommend leaders use an "economic linkages" worksheet to determine the return on investment from undertaking specific activities to drive results in the Five Pillars. For instance, leaders often ask, "How much is this recognition program going to cost us?" The worksheet quantifies the cost and the benefit. I know that if an organization concentrates on reducing pressure ulcers, they'll have all the money they need for a better employee recognition program.

The goals set under each Pillar—Service, Quality, Finance, People, and Growth—are desired targets. What will it take under each Pillar to be excellent? Each organization needs to define excellence in its own marketplace. Each leader then sets the goal for the organization, facility, division, and department based on all of the Pillars. While every facility will set goals across all Five Pillars, some units or departments may not have goals under a particular Pillar or Pillars. This is explained further in chapter 9.

ON GETTING RESULTS

Excerpted from a note by an attendee at a Studer Group Institute

Mr. Studer,

When I spoke with you in Atlanta, you asked me to e-mail you my list of key learnings that I am taking back to my organization. Many leaders at my hospital have heard you speak so we have incorporated many of your suggestions into our operations already.

Throughout my 14 years at this hospital, I have worked in many clinical positions before I became a director. Fortunately for me, many of the tools you suggest were already in place by the time I had my current position.

The most important things you spoke about that I have personally seen work with tremendous results are:

• Rounding for Outcomes

• Key Words at Key Times with Key Actions

• The Pillars of Excellence

The point I would stress to other managers is that you can never overemphasize the importance of the little things like treating staff fairly, having kind words to say, and being your staff's biggest fan...and remembering that not only are the patients your customers, but so are their families, your physicians, and other employees.

Re-recruitment strategies couldn't be more important in light of the nursing shortage. By utilizing your suggestions, I have not only dropped the turnover of my department to 5% from 15–20%, but I have a waiting list of staff who want to work in my department!

Thank you for inspiring this Fire Starter,

Antonio
Director

I urge every health care organization to strive to be the best health care organization in the country. Not "good enough," but "the best." When I first emphasized this goal at Baptist, employees asked me, "Quint, didn't you mean best in the *county?*" I didn't. I meant best in the country.

Most hospitals are already good, but America needs *excellent* hospitals.

And I know that every hospital can be better, no matter how good it is. I see it in nursing all the time. One hospital thought they had achieved their ultimate RN turnover level when it fell to ten percent. They thought it couldn't get any better than that. But it did. It went to six percent. They found that the more staff they retained, the more staff they recruited. Retained employees recruited their friends! That's what a commitment to excellence does.

In such a culture, employees feel valued. They have input. They feel rewarded and recognized.

In such a culture, employees manage their own morale. Employees are in charge of their own happiness. You can't do it for them. You can create an atmosphere for the person to make good choices, but you can't make them happy.

When I had been president at Baptist for about three months, a lady approached me at the grocery store.

"Are you Quint Studer?" she asked.

I told her I was.

"Thank you," she said. "My husband is so happy when he comes home now. You don't know what that means to me."

"Thank him. Not me," I said. Because it was his decision to seek out job satisfaction. Not mine. Baptist was not a perfect place to work. In fact, I knew there were going to be days when he would come home not so happy. I didn't want her to come looking for me again when one of those days came! I didn't want credit for his bad mood. So I couldn't take credit for his happiness. And neither can you. It is still up to each individual to self-motivate.

When the Student is Ready, the Teacher Appears

No one can take credit for the professional development of others, either. Sometimes folks come up to me and say, "You really helped me." I say, "*You* helped you! I gave the same information to 30 people, but you used it."

Our mission at Studer Group is to make health care a better place for patients to receive care, employees to work, and physicians to practice medicine. Many leaders with heart and courage have joined us on the journey.

I remember a time when we began coaching a hospital on the outskirts of a major city surrounded by many hospitals. They asked us to sign a non-compete agreement. We explained that signing such an agreement would not be consistent with our mission to make health care better everywhere. While disappointed, they said they understood. They recognized that great service is a powerful competitive advantage. However, today we work with this hospital and *all* of the hospitals in the area—just as we do in other regions of the country. Today this hospital excels under all of the Five Pillars and now actively helps other area hospitals to hardwire excellence at their organizations.

One night two years ago, the home of this hospital's COO was invaded. During the break in, he was shot four times. He was rushed to the closest hospital (which was a competitor), where he lay in an induced coma for 42 days. During those 42 days, the administrative team from his hospital rotated so that someone was always present there. I guarantee you that as those leaders waited with their co-worker in intensive care, they wanted the very best care for him in the very best hospital. That's why our goal is to help all hospitals, medical centers, and clinics be the best. We never know where we or our loved ones will end up. Today, the COO is back at work. Making a difference. Better than ever.

HARDWIRING
EXCELLENCE

CHAPTER FOUR

◉

PRINCIPLE 2
MEASURE THE IMPORTANT THINGS

To achieve Five Pillar excellence, we find organizations must be able to objectively assess their current status and then track their progress to the goals they have set. Principle 2 helps organizations define specific targets, measure progress against those targets, and align the necessary resources to achieve them. In this chapter, I use patient satisfaction as an example of how to align goals and measure progress. The same approach is used across all Five Pillars.

KEY CONCEPTS OF MEASUREMENT

Measurement supports the alignment of desired behaviors. It excites the organization when goals are achieved. Measurement also holds individuals accountable for the results and helps to determine if things are working. **We are not measuring just to measure.** We are measuring to align specific leadership and employee behaviors (to be described in chapter 9) that cascade throughout the organization to drive results. The better an organization can align these behaviors, the more quickly it will achieve desired results and create opportunities to recognize staff. Recognized behavior gets repeated, which turns the Flywheel faster.

UTILIZING MEASUREMENT AS A DIAGNOSTIC AND PROCESS IMPROVEMENT TOOL

Here is one example of how measurement can drive results in patient satisfaction. In one hospital, an Emergency Department Leader divided up the hospital's patient satisfaction data by doctor. She met with each doctor individually and went over the patient satisfaction results for the physician, or as we like to say, "the patient's perception of their care." Physicians take great pride in providing quality care. So a doctor who had particularly low satisfaction asked her, "What are the physicians with the higher satisfaction doing that I am not?" She told him. And he got better.

Using the measurement tool, the nurse showed the doctor how he was perceived poorly by the patient in the category of "listening," which was critical to receiving higher patient satisfaction. She used the measurement data to communicate and align his behavior. She provided him specific tips, tools, and actions to be more successful. Equally important, she told him that she wanted him to be successful. A multiple win.

By looking at the data and adjusting the behavior, this leader improved results. I find that if finance people consider satisfaction data in the same way they would a profit-and-loss statement, they get it. In fact, finance people can be a great teaching resource for the organization on how to use metrics. The same holds true for clinicians when they begin to review patient surveys in the same way they would the results of a diagnostic test.

- They evaluate the current results based on data.

- They take action to improve results.

- They closely monitor results.

- And they report on what works and what doesn't.

Then they adjust the techniques they use and change prescriptions until they get the results they are seeking. Measurement is based on tracking and using indicators. As results improve, it ignites greater passion throughout the organization and turns the Flywheel.

This data also leads to process improvement. When I arrived at Baptist Hospital, Inc., the food service scores were in the high teens to low twenty's. I met with the leader to find out what the plans were to improve. The key question to ask a leader is not about what happened, but, "What actions are you taking to move us in the right direction?"

We all have compelling reasons for why something has been difficult to achieve. In this case, the leader mentioned staff cuts and a smaller budget for nutritional snacks. But as I looked at the data breakdown by unit, I noticed that on 3 East, scores were higher. To this individual's credit, he became a student of what was being done differently on 3 East. It turned out that they had the same issues as other units, but that 3 East had created a better process to pass out trays and explain diets. When all units adopted this process, food satisfaction increased all the way to 99th percentile. So it's not about not having the financial resources, but rather about how well you can spot best practices and how quickly you can adopt and transfer them throughout the organization.

How Measurement Aligns Behavior

When clear goals are combined with consistent measurement and aligned behaviors, results start to come. Individuals are more motivated and begin to understand the importance and power of the behaviors they are being asked to use. Momentum of results increases as success creates more success.

Here's an example of a note a coach received from one organization that changed behaviors with data:

Hello and Thanks!

I'm pretty pleased with the satisfaction scores . . . The ED physicians are finally on board, although a couple still have their moments. Dr. R. has truly taken ownership of his poor scores. In fact, he has moved from a score of 50% in March to 95% in August! He has truly turned himself around . . . and it all started when he agreed to "give it a shot . . . do what we said . . . and if it didn't work, then he would know for sure that it wasn't worth the effort!"

Not only is he a true believer now, but today I met with all the other physicians and explained how they needed to model their behavior after him! As requested, Dr. R. had written on the back of his business cards, "Thank you for allowing us the privilege of taking care of you and your family member. Our goal is to provide you with VERY GOOD care. I hope we were able to accomplish that goal." Now all the physicians are handing out such cards and requesting that patients please call them with questions or needs for further assistance.

Our "Morning Report" meeting with physicians and nurses in the lounge has also been a great success. We discuss announcements, positives, negatives, medical issues, and create a goal for the day. When we first started, I had to hustle everyone into the lounge and then guard the door so they wouldn't sneak out. Now there is a spirit of camaraderie and information exchange that we all look forward to. Everyone is assembled by the time I join them.

I have started hardwiring discharge call backs to patients, tracking how many calls a particular nurse has made and how many shifts she has worked. Then I meet with each one and share the information. Talk about lighting some fires! The patient satisfaction feedback we got in our call backs from July to August improved dramatically once the nurses caught on to the fact that I was tracking our progress individually and as a team.

Thanks for your encouragement and support,

Pat, Emergency Department Nurse Manager

How Often Do We Measure?

Principle 2 is a critical driver in a culture of service and operational excellence because what gets measured gets done. One of the most important things about measurement is to measure often enough so you can reward and recognize as soon as possible after the behavior occurs. Tracking patient satisfaction quarterly isn't frequent enough, in my experience. If I were trying to lose weight and someone told me I couldn't weigh myself for three months, I know I wouldn't be successful. I've got to see some progress a little quicker to stay motivated. Individuals who work in health care are focused people. We measure clinical progress often. And so we should with satisfaction data.

In 1993, a patient satisfaction survey company told me that if I wanted to measure so frequently, the data might not be statistically reliable and valid. But reliability was not my top priority. Changing behavior was. Trend data over many surveys will in fact be valid and reliable. But frequent measurement is most importantly a way to reinforce positive behavior. I am not suggesting you base big decisions upon a week's worth of data. But the data will add up, and trends will become evident.

By measuring often, process improvement increases and the hospital becomes a better organization.

Do you think the folks in accounting count the money once a quarter? Nope. They count once a day, and sometimes more often. Why? Because it's important to know the gains and the losses. It also allows staff to adjust focus as needed based on daily results. I think this is good.

Organizations should take a pulse frequently, whether for patients, financials, patient and employee satisfaction, or other key operations.

The more often we *measure the important things*, the more we'll know about where we are making progress and where we are not. And the more we know, the more we can affect behavior.

While there are many questions on a survey, some have more impact than others. In fact, the "key drivers" or "correlating coefficients" on the measurement surveys can drive the results in the Five Pillars. These are the questions that have the largest impact on patients' perception of care. Here is a focused approach that I recommend for leveraging results quickly from survey data: Choose one of the key driver questions and develop an action plan for improvement. This approach will not only lead to improvements in the particular issue that is being addressed, but it will also increase the overall perception of patient care.

Every leader should understand which questions are the most influential for patients' perception of care with respect to their areas. By creating a plan of action based on the highest impact questions for the department, leaders will maximize gains. Also, as staff members see the relationship between the actions they take and results they achieve, they will be ready to move to the next question. This is a great way to focus staff without overwhelming them with an exhaustive "To Do" list.

Remember to:

- Focus on opportunities to create desired behaviors — not just measurement.

- Act fast.

- Put the data to use.

- Push for results—not excuses.

I tell CEOs that all they have to do to have a successful hospital is to spend the same amount of time focusing on People, Service, Quality, and Growth as they already do on the Finance Pillar. There must be a willingness to give the other Pillars equally high priority and create action plans. How many months would you allow a leader to miss his or her budget without an action plan for change? When an organization treats results in all Pillars with the same seriousness and intensity as the Finance Pillar, all Pillars will improve.

INTERPRETING DATA CORRECTLY

In 1993 at Holy Cross in Chicago, our patient satisfaction score started off below the fifth percentile. So we formed a measurement team to see what we could do about it. They were excited about their mission. The measurement team helped us learn not only about the survey tool we were using but about which departments to focus on for improvement. For example, we learned that a raw score of 84 in food service was actually better than an 88 in nursing and so we needed to focus on improving nursing over food service. Why? Because when the raw scores were converted to percentile rankings compared to hospitals nationwide, the hospital's food service score would rank it high compared to other organizations food service areas, while our nursing score might rank lower compared to other organizations nursing scores. If raw scores for both meals and nursing are 80, food service would be in the 90th percentile and nursing would be at the 0 percentile compared to other hospitals.

In fact, I'll be forever grateful to our measurement team leader, Don Dean. One day as I was rushing off to a low-scoring area to spend 30 minutes on what I considered an urgent crisis, Don stopped me and said, "You know, Quint, the challenges in that area really don't have that significant an impact on the overall patient satisfaction, but nursing does."

He was right. Food, for instance, is important in a hospital. But if the food is average and the nursing is great, the family will recommend the hospital to others. If the food is great but the nursing is average, they will more likely not recommend the hospital to others. Here is why quality food service is important: If it is poor, the patient will complain to the nurse, which makes him or her less available for clinical care. Again, I'm not saying food is not important; it's just that many times nursing may be more important.

So instead of focusing on an area with less impact, Don sent me to visit each nursing unit that had improved and thank them. Measurement helped me to understand that the foundation of inpatient satisfaction is nursing. While all areas are important, nursing is vital.

Studer Group coaches organizations that use a wide variety of survey tools, but there appear to be four common drivers for patient satisfaction regardless of the tool that is used:

- Communication

- Pain Management

- Personal Needs

- Response to Call Lights

We know that organizations that focus on measuring and improving these four areas within nursing units will achieve excellent results with respect to patient satisfaction.

Moving from Good to Very Good — Find Out What Makes the Difference

I often find there is a temptation to focus on the patients who ranked their experience as poor on patient satisfaction evaluations. Instead, I recommend you focus on those patients who rated you good instead of very good—the second best rating—to learn how you can move them to very good.

Here's why: Many patient satisfaction tools feature a 1 (very poor) to 5 (very good) rating, where 5 is the best. The goal is to be the best, so if your survey instrument says that's a 5, work on moving more 4s to 5s. If it's a 10, shoot for that.

Again, don't spend too much time worrying about low scores. If you want your hospital to be ranked highly compared to others in your survey vendor's database, it's all about moving the 4s to 5s. Hospitals are so good already that if you get all 4's or "good's," you may be the lowest hospital in the database. You need to move scores from second best to best.

Here's how to find out what will make the difference: Call the patients who ranked you as "good." Say, "Thank you for completing the survey. We appreciate your saying that you received good care while at our hospital. What could we have done better to have earned a 'very good' rating from you (if that is the improvement mark)?"

Then call those who rated their experiences as very good and ask, "Can you tell us some things we did that helped you feel we were very good?" (Note: Use the words from the survey, e.g., replace "very good" with "very satisfied" or "excellent," based upon your survey instrument's top rating.)

There are even some organizations that are not satisfied with waiting until the patient's experience is over to find out what makes the difference. They are even more proactive. One North Carolina hospital I know asks the patient and family upfront, "What is most important to you during your stay with us?" or: "In order for you to be completely satisfied, what do we need to focus on in addition to the great clinical care you will receive?" Then if they say that they would really appreciate an extra pillow or coffee that is hot, make sure they get it. Don't guess. Ask them. The patient and their family will be appreciative. This organization sets a natural pace for great prescriptive care for the patients. Today this hospital is one of the best in the country.

No Secrets: The Thermometer Question

One day the Holy Cross measurement team approached me and said that we had moved all the way from the 5th up to the 14th percentile in patient satisfaction. The measurement team wanted to put a thermometer up in the cafeteria — sort of like the United Way does to track fundraising. They wanted to put "75th Percentile Patient Satisfaction" (our goal) up at the top of the thermometer, and to show how we had progressed from below the 5th percentile to the 14th.

They were excited. They showed me a very large thermometer that our employees, docs, and even some family members would see. I tried to listen in a nice way to their remarks, but to me it was obvious that this wasn't going to work. I explained to them that we couldn't put the thermometer up in the cafeteria because the community would see it. And we didn't want the community to know about our low patient satisfaction.

Once again, an employee brought me a moment of clarity. In a very nice way, she said, "But Quint . . . they already know. Who do you think is giving us those patient satisfaction scores?"

We put the thermometer in the cafeteria.

They were right. If you want to change the results, don't hide the measuring you are doing. When all of a sudden the thermometer went up to the 40th percentile, the whole hospital celebrated because they had watched that thermometer creep up! We shared a map with all employees of what we'd done to get there. The map also laid out the next steps for us to get to the 75th percentile. Then we surpassed that goal too.

I think there can be no secrets in an organization. Everybody has to share information. Unfortunately, most organizations don't share information widely. Every employee must be able to see how the hospital is doing across all Five Pillars. Everyone has to see all of the data. This helps staff better understand the power of their role in shaping change and supporting key actions so they can be part of the solution.

I also recommend that results be broken down at the unit level. Each department needs to see how they are performing and improving. If this doesn't occur, improvement will be slow or nonexistent. Otherwise, it's always that other unit that's the problem.

CONNECTING BACK TO PURPOSE

Often, when I hear leaders discussing their patient satisfaction results, they say, "Our (name of company) results are . . . " I strongly discourage this because it takes away from connecting to the patient.

When a patient receives a diagnostic test in the radiology department, do we say, "Here are your GE results, Phillips results, and Siemens radiology results"? In cardiology, are they using the name of the vendor?

I find as we discuss patient satisfaction measurement tools that it helps if we call it "patient perception of care" or "patient satisfaction," rather than using the name of the vendor. Once I asked a group of employees if they understood what every patient who completed our patient satisfaction survey shared in common. They all had been cared for at our organization. These are not vendor numbers, but people we have touched. They tell us how we did and how we can do better. Don't put a vendor name between you and your patients.

Here's a letter I was copied on recently from one manager to her staff. This leader understands how to communicate about results and focus on the positive . . .

> Well, guys, we have slipped a little bit in our patient satisfaction this week. For the week of 7/13/03 to 7/19/03 we had 14 responses returned. Our satisfaction was at the 44th percentile, which means 56% of all other hospitals were better than us.

Now don't get discouraged. It is normal to see these ups and downs. This was lower than we had been in the previous several weeks. We are still at the 61st percentile for this quarter, which is much better than we were this time last year.

This week our patients said we were better at letting their family be with them, they felt safe, the doctors took time to talk with them, comfort of the waiting room improved, and doctors were courteous.

Our patients said we slipped a little bit in how well their pain was controlled, staff caring about you as a person, informed about delays, and waiting time to see a doctor.

I will try and keep you updated weekly on these reports.

Once again thanks for all of your hard work.

Regina
Manager

Measurement provides the vital signs for an organization. To help a patient get better treatment, measuring patient care is crucial. So too with the Pillars. The metrics are vital to the development of a treatment plan for the organization. **But the key to remember is that our metrics represent a patient, a physician, and an employee.**

Sometimes at an organization, a leader will ask me, "Don't you think we are focusing too much on the numbers?" I remind them that those numbers—4s and 5s or 9s and 10s—represent a patient's appreciation for quick response to call lights, for keeping them clean and comfortable, and for communicating consistently and managing their pain. The key is to continuously tie back the purpose of measuring to the staff. Just as we focus clinically on a temperature of 98.6° Fahrenheit (because it represents a patient without a fever), so too can we review patient satisfaction ratings as a way to represent that we are doing a good job in areas that are important to the patient. So Principle 2, Measure the Important Things, is like a diagnostic tool that measures current results, and identifies opportunities to improve those patient perceptions of care. When we implement the action plans, re-measure and note improvement, we can celebrate!

ON PATIENT PERCEPTION OF CARE

Excerpted from a note by an ED director

> My name is Joan and I am currently the director of an Emergency Department, which doesn't particularly make me outstanding, but the indirect connection I have had with you does. It's because of that I wanted to thank you.
>
> As nurses, when we take care of patients, we use the "skills" we learned to do the "tasks." While we were trained how to start IV's and give medications, we never learned how to understand the patient's true expectations. Very often, we miss the underlying reason why a patient is truly in the ED. We miss that the mother and father of a sick child are angry—not because we didn't see the child quickly, but because they are truly in need of a good night's sleep.
>
> We all excel in treating the disease; in fact, the more acute the patient, the more exciting our work. But when we give what we feel is 150%, we get upset about complaints . . . because we entirely missed what the patient really needed.
>
> There aren't any classes offered in school that focus on this kind of service. Yet I believe it is just as important as giving the right medication to the right patient. Thank you for the revolution you have started. Your passion is contagious, and it's a disease I hope you continue to spread.
>
> Joan
> Director, Emergency Department

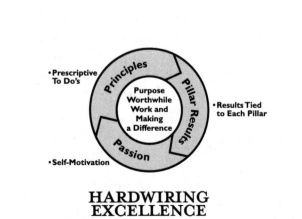

HARDWIRING
EXCELLENCE

CHAPTER FIVE

❦

PRINCIPLE 3
BUILD A CULTURE AROUND SERVICE

U sing Principles 1 and 2, we have set our goals, established how we are going to measure them, and committed to openly and frequently sharing information to improve.

In Principle 3, we want to define more prescriptive actions that will drive results. We also want to create enthusiasm for change because change isn't easy. We want to help out our leaders by getting staff on board early to engage them in the process. And we want to create systems and tools that will hardwire our focus on service: service to the employees, to the physicians, and to patients.

Principle 3, Build a Culture Around Service, teaches how to connect organizational values to actions through the use of employee-based service teams and two of Studer Group's six Must Haves™. They are: (1) **Key Words at Key Times** and (2) **Discharge/Post-Visit Phone Calls.** This ensures a high quality and caring environment for our patients, our employees, and physicians so we succeed in building a culture on operational excellence.

SERVICE TEAMS

A key way to drive process improvement and focus on service is to establish service teams. Through teams, we are engaging the employees to affect the culture and providing opportunity for action to create results. When employees see results, they understand and become more committed to change. The Flywheel will turn.

I also believe that it is the front-line staff who best know what needs to be fixed and how to do it. Through the team structure, we offer highly motivated employees the tools and resources they need to identify and solve key service and operational issues that cross over departments. Many times I have found that employees had good ideas for solutions, but we just didn't give them the opportunity to implement them.

Service teams help us harvest the good ideas. In chapter 8 on Principle 6 (Build Individual Accountability), I will lay out how we can take this to the next level through more systematic harvesting of intellectual capital.

TIP: Many people ask me which kinds of service teams they should form. My advice is to look at what you need to accomplish. For instance, most organizations have values statements, but they may not have very specific standards of behavior that clearly articulate how the employees will live out those values. This is an opportunity for a Standards Team to create them. Communication and reward and recognition are all organizational opportunities that are often cited on employee survey results as areas for improvement. Once you have evaluated opportunities in your organization and have formulated goals for achieving them, consider establishing some of the employee service teams below.

Here is a list of potential service teams and a brief description of each:

STANDARDS TEAM

Standards of behavior provide an important foundation for the organization as it establishes the code of conduct that all employees will live by. This team is responsible for developing the standards of behavior for all employees (e.g., "elevator etiquette," where staff will exit as necessary to make room for patients, or "commitment to co-workers," where each employee agrees to keep his work area clean as a courtesy to the next shift). The team also develops tools and rolls out strategies to ensure that employees fully understand and live by these standards.

PATIENT SATISFACTION TEAM

Typically, organizations establish up to four satisfaction teams: Inpatient, Outpatient, Medical Group, and the Emergency Department. These teams are responsible for ensuring that the highest level of service is consistently provided by their respective areas and for developing new ideas to continually improve that service and to share best practices among departments to help others learn. They are the evangelists for "WOW" service.

PHYSICIAN SATISFACTION TEAM

This team is responsible for ensuring that the highest level of service is consistently provided to physicians (for they are important customers) and for developing ideas to continually improve that service. They focus on removing irritants and identifying what the physician needs. The team also helps to deliver the message that physicians are valued partners in the delivery of care.

EMPLOYER OF CHOICE TEAM

This team is responsible to help the organization become an employer of choice, where employees feel they are doing worthwhile work, making a difference, and finding purpose in their jobs. They focus on implementing employee selection and orientation processes, employee forums, town halls, and employee survey action plans.

MEASUREMENT TEAM

This team is responsible for correctly measuring/interpreting data and communicating progress against patient satisfaction scores. Digging into the patient satisfaction measurement tool, they become the in-house experts and develop user-friendly easy-to-read reports, so that all staff know what their scores are on a timely basis. They work closely with all satisfaction teams so that they know how to read the reports and can identify trends, areas for improvement, and wins!

SERVICE RECOVERY TEAM

This team is responsible for developing service recovery policy for those patients whose expectations have not been met and for educating leaders and employees on how to use service recovery scripts and tools. The team's goal is to ensure that, when an employee hears a problem from a patient, they feel empowered to "own" it.

COMMUNICATION TEAM

This team is responsible for "connecting the dots" for employees to ensure that employees understand the reasons for and efforts behind establishing a culture of service and operational excellence. They help improve or build upon current communication vehicles that tell the story of going from good to great, including communication boards, newsletters, and employee town meetings. They work closely with the other teams to ensure they are getting their messages out and develop communications that can be used by all teams.

REWARD AND RECOGNITION TEAM

This team is responsible for developing processes and ideas that help the organization build reward and recognition into the daily practices of leaders and employees. Creating instant recognition programs, ensuring that leaders are using available reward programs, and celebrating achievements are a few of their areas of focus. The team also works closely with senior leadership and the service teams as an internal resource for reward and recognition ideas.

There are a number of other teams that I've seen in place at excellent organizations around the country. Don't be afraid to create new teams for specific purposes. Also, don't feel that a team has to be a permanent thing. What will endure is the tremendous appreciation that employees have for making a difference through these teams. These teams will create, identify, fix, and provide many positive influences.

Having listed the teams, let me share examples of the work of a few key teams.

BEGIN WITH THE STANDARDS TEAM

The most important team to start with is the Standards Team. If we are going to reach our goals, it will be the standards of behavior that get us there. In looking at employee attitude surveys, one of the things that usually jumps out is inconsistent performance in the workplace. We need to change that.

The Standards Team will help create standards for excellent behavior. That way, employees, physicians, and patients will demonstrate consistent behavior. In considering standards your organization will develop, I recommend that you look at the questions on your employee attitude surveys, patient satisfaction surveys, and physician satisfaction surveys. These survey instruments were developed by research companies based on what those three groups are impacted by the most.

We can use standards to align our behavior to outcomes identified in those survey tools (e.g., if ratings are poor on the survey question: "Staff listened to and answered all my questions," a communication standard would be to listen to and answer questions. We would create key words at key times to address this issue, such as: "Mrs. Johnson, we want to make sure we listen to and answer all your questions. Do you have any questions I can answer at this time?"). An organization will know it has succeeded when its survey results reflect that alignment. In other words, patient perception of care has improved because of the behavior standard that all employees are consistently using.

When developing behavior standards, a good question to ask is "In order for us to demonstrate standards of behavior to our co-workers, our patients, and our physicians, what does our behavior need to look like?" Try to be as specific as possible. For example, one standard may be to always introduce yourself when you are with a patient. Others might include always knocking prior to entering a patient room and asking permission to enter or closing a curtain completely and using the key words "I'm closing this curtain to ensure your privacy and confidentiality."

After the Standards Team has developed a rough draft of potential behavior standards, expose it to a larger sphere of influence. For example, one hospital sent their draft standards to every employee in the organization and asked for input. Fifty percent of the employees sent back input!

Another hospital we work with took the draft standards and posted them on the walls of the cafeteria. When employees entered the cafeteria, they shared their input by using colored stars. Green ones indicated behaviors they thought were absolutely imperative, yellow was for proposed standards they were okay with, and red was for the ones they disagreed with.

By involving staff, we are not only establishing consistent standards but also creating buy-in from the organization — building employee investment in the standards they will be asked to model.

A side note: Allowing employees with a bad attitude to work in the organization is a morale killer. When leaders begin to hold employees accountable for their attitudes and ask those to leave who do not meet the standards of behavior, organizations experience a huge boost in all Pillar results. Why? Once we ask poor performers to leave the organization, teamwork and interdepartmental relationships improve. This leads to more efficient operations. More staff become willing to align their behaviors to Pillar goals, and this in turn leads to better bottom-line results.

We recommend that employees be required to both read and sign a commitment to the standards of behavior. Make it part of the employee application process. Likewise, the standards also should be used in the discipline process. If employees are not following the standards, this should be addressed, just as if it were a medication error or absenteeism.

For many leaders, this is the first concrete process they have ever had to implement with employees who are technically good but are difficult to get along with.

MEASUREMENT TEAM DIAGNOSES CHALLENGES AND OPPORTUNITIES

The Measurement Team was designed to look at how we measure satisfaction and is a key team to utilize early in shaping a new culture, as discussed in Principle 2. Team members should represent a cross-section of leaders and employees.

The team should focus first on the patient satisfaction reports. In fact, since many of your employees have probably never seen the survey tool itself, the team should ensure that every employee receives a hard copy of the survey.

The team leader must clearly understand what questions are most important to patients and break the scores down at the unit level. Then the team must communicate these results hospital-wide.

By communicating it throughout the hospital, every leader knows everyone's results. I think this creates an open culture. It helps everyone know who is doing a good job. It also helps the ones who are struggling to know whom they can learn from.

The Measurement Team's work is not to provide the treatment but the diagnostic work, much like a radiologist. The Measurement Team will be able to identify an area that the hospital needs to improve in (like faster response to call lights) because of its importance to the patient. The team will be able to identify a nursing unit which has a low score in a particular area (e.g., food scores) and another that has high scores. The lower units can then benchmark the higher units. That leads to process improvement.

The Measurement Team's goal is to understand how the organization is doing, by unit, by question. This team should know if the organization is trending up or trending down. They should identify ways to communicate this information on a user-friendly basis. In fact, the information they provide becomes the foundation for leaders throughout the organization to harvest best practices; ask for action plans in areas that are not trending correctly; and reward and recognize top performers.

THE PHYSICIAN SATISFACTION TEAM BRINGS PERSPECTIVE

The main purpose of the Physician Satisfaction Team is to determine what physicians want and to better understand what they are frustrated about in the hospital. After spending time with the physicians and their office staff, this team often tells administration, "If we experienced these frustrations, we'd be more upset than they are." Seeing things from the physician's perspective is one of the goals of the team. I find that physicians are essentially seeking four things:

- Quality

- Efficiency

- Input

- Appreciation

Often organizations conduct small focus groups of physicians and ask, "In order for this to be a hospital that you absolutely want your patient in instead of anywhere else, please identify one or two things which would make this a better place for you to practice medicine and your patients to receive care."

We find physicians are happy to help. Usually the problems can be fixed. And then we communicate this to the physicians. Now the physicians are getting what they asked for — quality of care for their patients, efficient operations, appreciation, and input. Those are multiple wins for a single action.

TIP: FOCUS, FIX, AND FOLLOW-UP

Once you get a win, it's important to sustain the gain. Many times, we get a win with the physician, but then we go on to something else. Instead, we need to continue to harvest wins with the physicians, time after time, by focusing on the problem, fixing it, and following up by explaining how we were responsive to their need.

This is very valuable because it helps us to document with the physician that we understand and appreciate their goals. Once physicians are on board

---

with what and how we are measuring, and we are providing the physician with consistent data on progress, we will outperform their expectations in areas of which they have been historically critical (e.g., "O.R. is always late"). When we point out an area that needs improvement and suggest a plan to fix it, they perceive us as proactive in our physician communication instead of reactive.

We call this process Focus, Fix, and Follow-up. You can read more about it on our website *www.studergroup.com* under Articles: **Getting Physicians on Board.**

The great thing about physicians is that they will tell you where they feel the hospital can improve. For instance, one of the key irritants for physicians is when staff call physicians about a patient but do not have their chart on hand. Why? Inevitably, the physician will ask a question and the staff will ask the physician to wait while they get the chart. What does this say to the doctor about how the staff values his or her time? Many physician satisfaction teams have helped staff hardwire key actions to take before they call a physician. The team also helps connect for staff why these actions are so important to physicians.

A "Calling Physicians Card" that is displayed in nurses' stations for nurses to use is one of our most popular tools. It includes a checklist of tasks to be completed before calling on a physician. Another organization took it to the next level by establishing different guidelines by physician specialty for what information to have available before calling such a physician. What do we accomplish when we take such actions? The physician feels staff respect his or her time. The physician feels that their patients are in good hands. The physician feels good about the hospital and so is more willing to work with the organization in process development. They have confidence that the hospital will be responsive to their ideas. And when they believe the hospital is better run, they will want more of their patients to receive care there.

On Leading Teams

Since many team leaders will be managing multidisciplinary teams of people who don't report to them directly, we highly recommend team leader training. It's one thing to manage individuals whom a leader schedules and rates on performance evaluations. But it's a completely different experience to manage individuals when one has no influence on these things.

One tool that helps team leaders is asking each individual in attendance to verbally rank the team meeting on a scale from 1 to 10 in front of the group before they leave. This forces each individual to be accountable for his or her opinions. If they didn't feel the meeting was effective, they must say so. Otherwise, they lose credibility with the group when they later complain about the meeting to group members.

TIP: Rimmerman's Rules

Meeting guidelines can also be useful in creating focus, discipline, and individual ownership among team members from multiple disciplines who don't typically work together. Dr. Curt Rimmerman, a cardiologist who leads a service team at the Cleveland Clinic Foundation, developed a set of meeting guidelines which have come to be known affectionately there as "Rimmerman's Rules."

They are:

• Leave rank at the door.

- No whining.

- Contribute at least one "bright idea" per session.

- No "sidebar" communications allowed.

- If you have something to say, say it in the room.

- Assume that each person wants to be here.

- Identify problems and focus on solutions.
  (Input — Discussion — Decision)

- Review the objectives before we leave to ensure they are realistic in scope.

- Leave with a sense of accomplishment
  (purpose, making a difference).

- Expect work outside of the meeting through sub-groups and task forces.

Service Teams Help Us Do Things Differently to Get Different Results

Someone once told me the definition of insanity is doing the same things over and over and expecting different results. Service teams help us change by harvesting the creativity of energetic, enthusiastic employees who want to make a difference in the lives of their patients, co-workers, and physicians. And they facilitate staff taking ownership by identifying problems and finding solutions.

These are all important reasons to look to service teams to build momentum in the Flywheel, but the team cannot keep it turning long-term without leaders who are committed to cascading their recommendations throughout the organization.

In fact, service teams are so wonderful that I notice some organizations count too much on them to drive change. A word of warning: While this will be effective in the short-term, it will only work over the long-term if leaders are consistently developing their skill sets to increase competencies through regular leadership development training, and organizations are using an objective leadership evaluation tool. If they are not, these improved processes and systems are at risk and may not be sustainable.

That is why chapter 6, Principle 4, focuses on developing and creating leaders, one of the most critical elements to achieving and sustaining long-term results. And, since each department is different, the leader will need to develop their own list of actions to drive results in their areas.

Some of the key "Must Haves" for leaders and service teams are **"Key Words at Key Times"** and **"Discharge/Post-Visit Phone Calls."**

KEY WORDS AT KEY TIMES

◀ MUST HAVE ◀

In building a culture on service and operational excellence, it is critical to let the patient, staff, and physician know why we do things. They want to know what is going on. They want us to connect the dots. We do this by using **Key Words at Key Times.**

For example, if you have curtains between beds and you walk into the room and pull the curtains closed without saying anything, what's the patient going to think about that? Anything he wants to:

- He might think you're rude.

- He might think you are trying to hide something.

Every day, thousands of curtains get moved. How many times is there an explanation to go along with this action? Here's what we recommend. When you close the curtains, say:

"Mrs. Medley, we want to make sure you have privacy here at our hospital. Let me close these curtains for you."

A patient will often associate closed curtains with a hospital that cares. That's an example of **Key Words at Key Times.** However, you can also test key words with patients by asking permission, such as: "Ms. Medly, would you like me to close these curtains?" (Note: Using key words also gives patients an opportunity to respond and share their preferences and needs with you. If you offer to close a door for privacy, for instance, one patient may express gratitude while another may say he feels less lonely when he hears friendly voices in the hallway.)

KEY WORDS AT KEY TIMES ALSO HELP POSITION DOCTORS WITH PATIENTS.

For example, my father traveled to the Cleveland Clinic Foundation to see a cardiologist. The experience was a little intimidating for him. It's a big place. Over 14,000 employees work on one campus. He sat in a waiting room with heart transplant patients. And he had to sit there for a while.

I knew the cardiologist was an excellent doctor. When he went to the exam room, Rebecca, the R.N., walked in and said: "Mr. Studer, you're a very fortunate man. You have an appointment with Dr. Young, He's one of the best cardiologists in the world."

How's my dad feeling now? Pretty good. Rebecca was able to erase a lot of Dad's anxiety with those few key words.

I believe, especially in office practice settings, that most nurses truly believe the doctors they work with are good physicians and provide quality care. They want to do worthwhile work, have purpose, and make a difference in the lives of patients. And if they believe a doctor is not clinically good, then they won't work there.

I know of hospitals that feel key words are so important that they devote entire meetings to developing key words to position doctors favorably. This can be used in a variety of activities.

For example, if I'm doing your lab draw, I can say to you:

"Mr. Brewer, Dr. DeCampos cares about you very much and wants to make sure we do this blood draw so your lab results will be available when she comes to the hospital. I have five years of experience and have taken thousands of blood draws. May I look at your arm? I know this isn't a pleasant experience, but I have had advanced training to make this as easy as can be on you. Let me also check your wrist band. Patient safety is very important to us."

How does Mr. Brewer feel about his doctor? Good. Why? Because she cares about him and is thinking about him.

How does Mr. Brewer feel about his lab draw? He's comfortable with it.

How does he feel about patient safety? He feels secure.

What if I had said:

"Mr. Brewer. Whoa! I'm glad I'm not you. Would you look at the size of this needle? I hope you have some pretty high tolerance to pain. Uh oh. I see your veins are small! This may take a few tries."

Or what if I just came in without saying anything and grabbed your arm?

Key Words at Key Times with key behaviors make all the difference in the world.

We've also found that unless you are very direct with questions, patients won't ask about their concerns. So before they leave a patient's room, at many hospitals the staff say:

"Is there anything else I can do for you? I have time."

If they don't ask this, what happens? The patient waits for a few minutes and then hits the call button. Or the patient never asks but instead complains to family members. We have found that the top three reasons patients use call lights at hospitals are for toileting assistance, positioning needs, and pain medication requests.

So the best way to reduce patients' use of call buttons is to anticipate unmet needs. Are the bedside table, telephone, call light, tissue, and trash can all within reach? Use key words that set patient expectations about when a nurse will return to the room. For instance, you might say, "Miss Adams, is there anything else I can do for you? I've moved your table so the phone and pain medication are easier to reach. And you've just been to the restroom, so I plan to be back in two hours, at 3:00. If you need me before then, please just call."

Doctors are the best at **Key Words at Key Times** because they've been practicing them for years. After they've examined a patient, they say:

"Before I leave, do you have any questions?"

And:

"I want you to know I'm available. The nurses know how to get in touch with me. If you need anything, you just let them know."

Why do they do that? First of all, they save a lot of time by asking before they leave. Secondly, they know this will make their patient feel a lot better. So they do it out of both efficiency and concern.

When I speak to audiences of health care employees, I ask: "Have any of the nurses ever been called back into a patient's room because the patient felt that housekeeping missed something?"

They always answer: Yes!

So, let's talk about how **Key Words at Key Times** with key behaviors can not only raise patient satisfaction but also increase staff productivity. A housekeeper, for example, asks:

"Is your room clean for you?"

"Did I miss anything?"

"Is there anything I can do before I leave?"

When a housekeeper uses key words, he or she has increased personal productivity. Why? Because now, if a patient needs something, they will ask for it at the outset. But if the key words are not used and the patient is not asked, what happens? The patient asks for it later, and the housekeeper is called to come back to the unit.

A housekeeper's key words also increase the efficiency of the nurse, because who is called when the patient needs something? The nurse. And the nurse has to call housekeeping and explain what's needed. Using **Key Words at Key Times** with key behaviors eliminates this wasted time.

WHICH KEY WORDS TO DEVELOP

It's best for you to develop your own **Key Words at Key Times.** Your survey tool will help in the development. For example, if you see that your patients have rated you lower than you would like on being responsive to their needs, you can sit down with your staff and help them determine what they can be doing and saying to give the patients that assurance.

ON KEY WORDS AT KEY TIMES

Excerpted from a note from a hospital employee

> I just wanted to share my thoughts with you regarding the changes and expectations that Studer Group introduced to our staff.

> First of all, change is sometimes difficult to accept. It's not that we don't want to accept it, but sometimes as employees we just don't see the reason behind the change. I must say that when I first heard of some of the things they wanted us to say at our hospital (such as "I have the time" and "Is there anything else I can help you with?") I laughed along with more than a few others.

We thought you must be kidding! Not that we wouldn't want to help as much as we could, but to verbally announce that we have the time . . . Well, we just felt it didn't make sense.

I must admit though, after seeing how patients and families react to these words, I have personally seen how it makes a difference. Patients seem to relax and feel more at ease. When I introduce myself, they seem more tapped into the registration process. And when I ask if there is anything else I can do for them—even if it is where is the restroom or gift shop—I see how it helps them tremendously. Letting them know that we have the time and truly want to help them really makes a difference.

Carolyn
Registration clerk

Except for basic organizational key words such as "How may I help you?" most departments create their own customized key words.

Admitting is a good area for key words. If people are afraid to enter the hospital, perhaps we should help. When I was a hospital president, we asked the Admitting Department to develop key words that would reassure new patients and their families. When the department staff got together and reviewed the survey tool, they saw how it measured whether they showed courtesy and skill. They came up with this:

"Good morning, Miss Land. Our goal is to provide you with excellent care. What may I do for you today?"

Here's an example of how key words are also important for a Personal Nursing Assistant (PNA). A PNA can be more effective by using a series of key words to make the patient feel more comfortable, to ensure that the patient is satisfied, and to help the patient contact the PNA instead of the nurse when personal needs arise. Consider the following conversation:

"Hello, Mr. Lloyd. I'm Norm Adams. I'm your personal nursing assistant. I want to make sure that you're very satisfied with your hospital care, especially your personal needs, such as taking a bath."

He continued: "I know it's uncomfortable having other people take care of you, but that's really what I'm here to do. If there's any time when you need any of your personal needs addressed, please let me know. In fact, every time I come into your room, I'll be checking with you about your needs. Is there anything I can do for you right now? I have time."

By using a series of key words, this PNA has helped Mr. Lloyd understand his role and has already begun to increase his satisfaction. He knows the PNA is there to help him with needs he might be uncomfortable in addressing.

If Mr. Lloyd is in Med/Surg, the RN will use key words to manage up Norm, the PNA, and continue to increase this patient's satisfaction:

"Hello, Mr. Lloyd. I'm Barbara. I'm your nurse for this evening. Mr. Lloyd, as you know, we want to make sure you're very satisfied with the care you receive at our hospital. And your personal needs are very important to us. I see you have Norm as your personal nursing assistant. He's excellent. Has Norm talked to you about your personal needs? Good. He will do a great job for you. I know you'll be very pleased."

Barbara will use these key words with each of her patients. She will also tell Norm what an excellent job he's done in talking to the patients. In so doing, she is recognizing his behavior and is re-recruiting him. So the patient is better. The nurse can focus on the treatment. And the personal nurse assistant (PNA) can focus on preventing pressure ulcers and maintaining cleanliness. The nurse is more effective. The PNA recognizes the impact of their important role and is even recognized by staff. A win-win-win.

TIP: A GREAT TOOL FOR KEY WORDS

I have found that regardless of what area you work in, The Five Fundamentals of Service or A-I-D-E-T provides a good framework to apply **Key Words at Key Times.**

A stands for "Acknowledge the patient." You want to acknowledge them by their last name if possible.

I is for "Introduce." Introduce yourself, your skill set, your professional certification, and your training: "Hello, Mr. Clark. My name is Jackie and I'm a medical technologist. I will be taking your X-ray today. I have been a medical technologist for 10 years. In fact, I've done this procedure hundreds of times and I go back for additional training each year. I also have certification from the *American Registry of Radiologic Technologists.*"

D is for "Duration." Describe the test: how long it's going to take; how long they're going to be there; and how long they'll have to wait on the results.

E stands for "Explanation." Explain the tests, the pain involved (be very honest), and what happens next. Explain you are going to be looking at their wrist band and why. Connect key words with patient safety and excellent care.

T stands for "Thank you." "Thank you for choosing our hospital."

These are the five fundamentals to create very satisfied patients. If you do all five of these fundamentals, your patient satisfaction will be a 5. If you do four of the five, you're a 4. It's the difference between good and great.

Key Words at Key Times is a powerful Must Have. **Key Words at Key Times** can help with re-recruitment, with personal needs, patient satisfaction, and the list goes on and on. They increase patient satisfaction while decreasing call lights, to raise efficiency. That means nurses are gaining time. And that's hardwiring for excellence!

DISCHARGE PHONE CALLS OR POST-VISIT CALLS ◄MUST HAVE◄

Another key driver of patient satisfaction is discharge or post-visit phone calls.

Research shows that confusion over discharge instructions is one of the top eight patient dissatisfiers. In the February 2003 issue of *Annals of Internal Medicine,* the authors describe just how vital care is in the first 72 hours after discharge. **Discharge follow-up phone calls allow the staff to re-connect after the patient has left the hospital or office setting. In organizations that are consistently achieving the best results in patient satisfaction, the patient is contacted 24 to 48 hours after discharge.**[1]

However, I do not recommend making discharge follow-up phone calls until after an organization has implemented **Rounding for Outcomes**. If I go up to a nurse and ask her to make a follow-up phone call to a patient, but she doesn't have the blood pressure cuffs she needs and nobody is helping her to fix systems that make it difficult for her to deliver quality care and she doesn't feel appreciated, then she will not be receptive to making **Discharge Phone Calls**.

In chapters 7 and 11, I will explain how we can build this emotional bank account through the use of **Rounding for Outcomes** and **Thank You Notes.** When Jackie, a nurse, gets the tools and equipment she needs and a thank you note, the next time I ask for something from her, I will usually get it. When I ask her to make some **Discharge Phone Calls**, she will be cooperative.

In fact, just as I suggested the focus, fix, and follow-up approach with physicians, I'd say, "Jackie, I see you got the blood pressure cuffs you needed. Is that helping? Good. Jackie, would you mind making a couple of phone calls a day to patients who have been discharged? We want to see how they're doing. We also want to make sure they are following their discharge orders and to make sure their clinical outcomes are improving. And we want to understand how they feel about the hospital and what we could do better."

In other words, I'm asking Jackie to:

1. Demonstrate empathy.

2. Improve clinical outcomes.

3. Harvest reward and recognition for the staff.

4. Learn about the patient's perception of service.

5. Gather process improvement suggestions.

Will Jackie do it? I am betting she will.

How to Conduct the Call

Creating a discharge follow-up phone call system is an evolutionary process. As I mentioned, in the initial phase of this process, the important thing is for somebody to make the call. It could be a volunteer. A simple process to implement is to have the unit clerk copy the discharged patient's face sheet before forwarding to medical records. Whoever makes the phone call is able to use this sheet as a guide. Ideally, an RN will make the call.

The first thing to do with a discharge phone call is to have EMPATHY and CONCERN.

"Mrs. Sengstock? Hi. This is [name]. You were discharged from my unit yesterday. I just wanted to call and see how you're doing today."

And then I'm going to listen.

Next, I move to CLINICAL OUTCOMES.

"Mrs. Sengstock, did you get all your medications filled?"

"Do you have your follow-up appointment?"

Then I ask about PAIN. "Is your pain better or worse than yesterday?" This might not always be an appropriate question. It depends on what they were in the hospital for.

I ask about DISCHARGE or HOME-CARE FOLLOW-UP ORDERS.

"Mrs. Sengstock, we want to make sure we do excellent clinical follow-up to ensure your best possible recovery. Do you understand your discharge instructions?"

Many times when people leave the hospital, there's so much going on that they do not understand what they are supposed to do when they get home. I recommend that you build questions about discharge orders into your phone call for several reasons:

1. When the patient receives home-care instructions, he may be too nervous or sick to ask questions.

2. Questions most often occur after the patient goes home.

3. All of the major survey tools ask questions about home care. The questions address patient satisfaction issues that can increase patient satisfaction scores, but the main point is still that discharge follow-up calls represent good care.

In working with many hospitals over the last few years, the biggest change I have noticed in the way **Discharge Phone Calls** are implemented is that organizations are no longer just using them to increase patients' perception of care, but to impact clinical outcomes, harvest staff recognition, audit the patient's perception of their care, and improve processes based on patient feedback.

A number of organizations now rely on their nursing staff to review discharge summaries to ensure that the patient is complying with home-care instructions and optimizing recovery. In these cases, the nurse can even help expedite a process if the patient is having problems following through on certain actions.

By optimizing clinical outcomes through **Discharge Phone Calls,** re-admissions and ER visits decrease.

A good way to turn discharge follow-up phone calls into something the staff likes to do is to add a question that allows the patient to recognize someone in the organization. This is a great opportunity to harvest REWARD AND RECOGNITION.

You might say: "Mrs. Sengstock, we like to recognize our employees. Who did an excellent job for you while you were in the hospital?"

This information provides an opportunity to reinforce desired behaviors with employees. Recognized behavior gets repeated.

Mrs. Sengstock might say, "You know that nurse Sue? She was just excellent!"

Then I might say, "Can you tell me why Sue was excellent?"

If possible, I want to capture the behavior that had an impact on the patient because we want to create our culture based on those behaviors. I want to be able to tell a nurse, "We called Mrs. Sengstock and she was very complimentary of you and said how much she appreciated your asking if there was anything else you could do for her." I want to recognize the behavior I want to see repeated.

During the call, I'd also ask, "Were there any physicians whom you'd like to see recognized?"

"Oh, wow! Dr. Frank was just marvelous! He came into my room at nine at night to see how I was doing."

Then, I'm going to find Dr. Frank and tell him what the patient said. In so doing, I'm providing positive input to a physician who so often hears negative feedback from hospitals. We don't compliment our physicians enough. We assume they don't need it, but they do. All of us need to feel recognized.

I also want to ask about PERCEPTION OF SERVICE.

"We want to make sure you were very satisfied with your care. How were we, Mrs. Sengstock?" I'd say. If they say it was great, I want to find out why it was great.

The last question will be one about PROCESS IMPROVEMENT.

"Mrs. Sengstock, we're always looking to get better. Do you have any suggestions for what we could do to be even better?"

In this discharge phone call, I've covered all the bases: empathy, clinical outcome, recognition, service, and process improvement. This simple phone call, hardwired into the system, will drive the organization to higher levels of service and reinforce behaviors we want to see repeated.

Using this sequence, we're finding out how the patient is first, before we ask how our care was. Our first two questions are focused on the patient. Our third question is based on the staff. The fourth question is based on our service. And the fifth question is based on our improvement.

One of the biggest challenges for organizations using **Discharge Phone Calls** is that they don't connect back to process improvement and reward and recognition. You have to use the information you capture to do a better job with patients in the hospital and to reward and recognize staff so the behaviors get repeated.

I have also found that hospitals are using **Discharge Phone Calls** in other areas, not just the inpatient settings. One system we coach is applying the concept of **Discharge Phone Calls** to their regional physician offices. Every new patient receives a call after their office visit. This allows them to capture the opportunities for improvement, as well as reward and recognition opportunities.

In summary, I have found that when organizations think about **Discharge Phone Calls**, they can become too focused on developing a perfect system instead of focusing on getting started. In health care, there can be a tendency to make things more complicated than they need to be. For **Discharge Phone Calls**, remember there is a natural progression that organizations can go through in developing a system. You might not be ready to do them completely the way I have described. So just start doing them, and the rewards will motivate the organization to continue to develop the **Discharge Phone Calls** in the ways I've described.

You cannot leave the phone calls to chance. In order for the organization to reap the rewards of **Discharge Phone Calls**, they must be hardwired so that every discharged patient gets called.

At hundreds of organizations, discharge follow-up phone calls are proving to have a huge impact. They are a valuable tool in making a difference in the lives of those we serve and can also have a powerful impact on the staff who make the calls.

WHAT DISCHARGE PHONE CALLS TAUGHT ME

Excerpted from a note to me by a Studer Group coach

> For me, the highlight of my day was a story one of the charge nurses shared with me after I presented the Nine Principles. She said that everything I had said about **Discharge Phone Calls** was true.
>
> When she was first told she would have to do them she pushed backed by saying she didn't have the time when

really she was concerned about getting a lot of complaints. But then she found the patient feedback to be overwhelmingly positive and came to enjoy them.

But she wanted me to know that she had gotten some negative feedback. In fact, one call in particular had changed her thinking about the calls. One patient said that his stay was very good except for the day of his discharge. The patient complained that the discharge nurse was in a big hurry and he felt like she was trying to "get rid of him."

The nurse was appalled that this would happen. So she pulled the patient record to see who his discharge nurse had been. Imagine her shock when she realized that SHE was the discharging nurse. She remembered the day. It had been busy, with an ED overflowing with patients waiting to be admitted.

She acknowledged that she was busy, but she never realized that the patient interpreted her busy-ness as wanting to "be rid" of him. She told me she was grateful for that feedback, since it gave her the opportunity to change her behavior—an insight she would never have had if not for the call. She said that that one call made every discharge call worth it!

I appreciate her maturity and willingness to look in the mirror and realize that she had to change.

Lucy

CREATING A SERVICE CULTURE

To create the culture, we have to make sure we know what the patients want and don't want. We need to know their concerns and structure our **Key Words at Key Times** with key behaviors. We need to connect with patients after they have left our organization through **Discharge Phone Calls**. We need employees to know and follow the standards of behavior to ensure consistency.

Why I Gave Patients My Home Phone Number

Building a culture on service teaches how to connect behaviors back to our organizational values. When I was president of a hospital, my goal was to role model the same behaviors I was asking others to do and thus be part of the patient care team. One such way was that each patient received a letter from me when they entered the hospital:

> Dear Patient,
>
> Welcome. We want to make sure you're very satisfied with the care you receive. If at any time you're not very satisfied with your care, please let us know. All of our staff are committed to your care. If you need to talk to me for any reason, please call. My office phone number is _____ and my home phone number is _____. We again want to make sure that we provide you and your family with the very best of care.
>
> Yours in service,
> Quint Studer
> President

I wanted the nurses to know that I wasn't telling them to do something while I was hiding. Once I put my home phone number on the letter, what did I communicate to the nurses? "I'm on the field."

It had another impact. I found that the nurses really didn't want the patients calling me. So this gave them an even greater incentive to make sure the patient was very satisfied.

By the way, I got about one phone call every 90 days.

I got this idea from a visit to Mountain Home, Arkansas. When I checked in at a small hotel there, I received a letter from the manager. He said that he wanted me to have a "10 experience" while I was there. He told me I would receive a survey when I left and he hoped I could give them a 10. He said in the course of my stay, if there was any reason I couldn't give them a 10, they'd like to know right away.

Then the manager said, "And if you need to talk to me at any time during your stay, here's my work number and here's my home number."

At the moment I read that, do you know what I thought? I thought, "Whoa! This is a good place! Because this guy would have to be a nut to give me his home number if it was a bad place."

So, I decided to do the same thing with a letter at our hospital.

I got a phone call one Sunday night from a lady who asked for "Quint Studer."

I said I was Quint.

She said, "I can't believe it. I thought this was some marketing gimmick the hospital was doing. My aunt is having heart surgery at your hospital. Are you guys any good?"

I said, "Well, I'm the president of the hospital so I'm probably going to say we are. But let me get Steve Cannon, the director of cardiovascular surgery, and if he's awake and if he can talk, I'll have him call you directly. And if he's not, I'll call you back."

I called Steve and he called her. At about 11:30 the next morning, my office called and said, "A lady you talked to on the phone last night stopped in. She said to tell you that everything was fine and to tell you 'thank you'."

A year later, I was at the Chamber of Commerce. They had invited me to come sit at a table for people with disabilities because it was Vocational Rehabilitation month. They asked me to say a few words, so I said, "My name is Quint Studer. I am the president of Baptist Hospital. On behalf of all the staff at Baptist, I would just like to guarantee you and your family that if you're at Baptist, everyone you come in contact with will say hello. We'll ask if we can help you and offer to take you where you are going. Before a staff member leaves you, they will say, 'Is there anything more I can do for you?'"

I sat down and a lady from the back of the room said, "What he said is true! My aunt had heart surgery about a year ago. I called him on a Sunday night at home because I was concerned about my aunt, and everything he just said the hospital would do, they did."

When a person stands up at a large Chamber of Commerce meeting and says those types of things to the community because she had access to my phone number . . . well, it creates wonderful word of mouth.

We found out that it doesn't matter to the patient if the hospital has a helicopter. It doesn't matter to the patient how many buildings you have. It doesn't even matter to the patient what your bond rating is. But what do matter are things like explaining about wait times, courtesy toward patients and family members, attention to personal needs, and getting a phone call after they have gone home.

A Physician's Appreciation for Quality Care

A letter from a physician to Martin Brotman, M.D., President and CEO of California Pacific Medical Center, San Francisco, CA

Dear Dr. Brotman,

I wanted to share with you my experience this past week.

I attended the funeral of one of our patients this past weekend. Josh was an eight-year-old boy who passed away last week after fighting advanced liver cancer for four months. The family was initially treated at another hospital, and after the patient failed conventional treatment they came to us for another try.

They spent the last two months with us heroically battling cancer until the end.

What touched me the most about this case and the funeral was the gratitude the family felt toward our hospital. I have always enjoyed my work here, and I believe that the pediatric team is truly exceptional. We deliver the best medical care in a compassionate and loving environment. What I learned this weekend is that this is also true everywhere else in the hospital.

I had several family members come up to me and tell me how grateful they were for the care, how wonderful everyone was. They mentioned the people that cleaned the room who always had a kind word; Chef Joseph who came up every week to check if he could make anything special for Josh; the radiology techs who were kind and gentle; the people who came up with the courtesy cart every day and showed kindness to the family; the transport people who were gentle and sensitive. Even our security people (two of whom attended and spoke at the funeral) were mentioned as exceptionally kind and compassionate.

I guess it touched me ... what an incredible workplace this is. Usually the doctors and nurses get most of the credit and praise, but I learned this weekend that everyone who came in contact with this family gave them something and aided in their healing. Josh's mom mentioned specifically that he, on several occasions, mentioned how much he liked this hospital (not something an 8 y/o boy says in the hospital).

To remind you ... this patient had spent a couple of months at another well-known hospital. Although I know he got great care there, all the family could remember was that the carpets were nice and the furniture was new. The compassion they got there could not compete with what we deliver daily.

I feel fortunate and grateful to be part of this place and humbled by the small role I play. As I put myself in the place of these parents—even for a moment—I am warmed by the thought that we provide the kind of care that we would want for our own loved ones if they needed it.

In the obituary from this weekend, this devastated family went out of their way to mention our hospital in their final memorial for their son.

Thanks for your time and please feel free to share this with anyone.

Yours truly,
Oded Herbsman M.D.
Medical Director, Pediatric Ward

That's what building a culture around excellence is all about. It serves a purpose. It makes a difference. It is worthwhile work.

1. *Annals of Internal Medicine, February 2003, p.95. "The Incidence and Severity of Adverse Events Affecting Patients after Discharge from the Hospital," by Alan J. Forester, MD, FRCPC, MSC; Harvey J. Murff, MD; Josh F. Peterson, MD; Tejal K. Gandhi, MC, MPH and David W. Bates, MD, MSc from Feb 4, 2003 Ann Inter Med. 2003 138:161-167*

CHAPTER SIX

PRINCIPLE 4
CREATE AND DEVELOP LEADERS

In order for an organization to be great, it has to have great leaders. In order to have great leaders, the organization has to invest in them. Principle 4 teaches how to develop, equip, and sustain courageous leaders to reach desired goals.

In 1999, I talked to a CEO from South Carolina whose employee turnover was very high. He said, "Quint, our employee turnover is high, and you have very low turnover at your hospital. What are you doing that I should do?"

I said, "First of all, look at your exit interviews and find out why folks are leaving. We also find taking leaders off-site to train them on employee selection, new employee orientation, and retention is crucial."

He said, "How long should we take them off-site?"

"We do a couple of days, every 90 days," I replied.

"Just can't do it," he said. "We just can't get them away for that long. They're too busy."

"What's your turnover?" I asked.

"It's 33 percent."

I said, "They may be too busy interviewing new employees."

Sometimes, because we don't deal with the cause, we get overwhelmed with the symptoms. Leadership training is at the heart of why employees want to come to work and why they want to stay. It's about the unit work environment and the supervisor. People don't leave their job. They leave the work environment. As I stated previously, the majority of employees leave their position because their relationship with their supervisor is not what they want it to be. Employees want to come to a place where they feel that they have purpose, are doing worthwhile work, and can make a difference. They want to feel a part of things. And they want to be recognized and appreciated. The supervisor holds the key to high employee retention.

Sometimes I get calls from people who attended one of our Institutes a year earlier, and they say, "Quint, we're doing everything you suggested at the Institute, but we're just not getting the results we hoped for."

I ask, "Are you training and developing your leaders?"

"Not really," they say. "That's the one thing we haven't done."

Then I ask, "Have you changed your leadership evaluation?"

"No, that's the other thing we haven't done."

The first 3 Principles will turn the Flywheel, but Principle 4, Create and Develop Leaders, and Principle 7, Align Behavior with Goals and Values, are what build momentum and sustain progress. **Whatever gains you get from the first 3 Principles will not be sustained without leaders who are continuously trained.** If you are not training and developing the leaders' skill set, they can't succeed. I don't believe that an organization can truly succeed at living its values (e.g., integrity, respect, teamwork, quality) without investing in developing the necessary leadership competencies. If organizations believe it's important to provide employees with the tools to be successful at their jobs, than the tools they should provide to leaders are leadership competencies. (Also of note: No Pillar gains can be sustained without the use of a solid leadership evaluation tool, explained in chapter 9, Principle 7.)

Why else are leadership competencies so important?

An organization can have a wonderful benefits package, but if a nurse leader doesn't know how to conduct a re-recruitment meeting, it won't work.

An organization can adopt standards of behavior, but if it hasn't trained a supervisor to confront problem employees, it won't work.

An organization can have great Pillar goals, but if a department leader doesn't know how to effectively communicate those goals at department meetings, it won't work.

An organization can have great certificates and prizes, but if a unit leader doesn't understand how to use reward and recognition to align behavior, it won't work.

When considering how to develop leaders, I want to talk about three key points:

- the phases of organizational change,

- how to move operational performance by having high-middle-low performer conversations, and

- how to build leadership competencies in general through Leadership Development Institutes (LDI).

ORGANIZATIONAL EVOLUTION

In developing leaders in your organization, it's important to recognize the phases of change that leaders will face. This allows us to make sure the leader has the competencies to move the department, unit, and organization through each phase. Otherwise, it's easy to panic. When runners train for a marathon, they get intense training and coaching—and so should your leaders.

A key component of this training is learning about and anticipating "The Wall." Leaders, like runners, must learn to recognize the feelings and the symptoms so they know when they are hitting The Wall and refrain from panic. If they have been well-coached, they will keep moving. What would a runner with no coaching do when they hit the wall? They would stop!

I think the runner analogy holds true for an organization building a culture of excellence.

Over the years, when speaking to leaders of organizations that we coach, I have heard a common concern. Leaders and employees often say they are worried that this too will be like all the other "change" programs or fads rolled out in past years. They remember countless times when they worked hard for a year or two until the organization slowly drifted away from that path.

If I were a leader and heard that we were about to embark on a new journey to excellence, would I be thinking, "Oh! This will be different"?

No, I'd set my watch and wait for a year or two to pass—confident that we'd be back to where we were before, with the latest program on the distant horizon.

As I studied why some organizations were able to sustain great results while others never did, I thought about the analogy of the marathoner—how in health care we have our own wall. We will either hit it and return to where we started, or we will move over it. **I think if there are only one or two things that you take away from this book, knowing how to anticipate the wall and get over it should be one of them.**

Let me explain what The Wall is and how to get over it. On this journey, there are five phases of evolutionary change in an organization. While The Wall appears in the middle, we need to know all of the phases to anticipate and move ahead.

THE FIVE PHASES OF ORGANIZATIONAL CHANGE

PHASE 1: The Honeymoon

What to Expect

- Sense of excitement

- Right "to do" list

- "Things will get better"

- Hope reigns

- Easy, quick fixes are implemented

The first phase is the honeymoon. This happens at the beginning. You're fired up. You're excited. Things are going to get better. There's hope. There are some quick fixes.

It's very similar to when you are in a new relationship. You just feel great. That is good. That is normal. You have the right "to do" list and begin building the foundation.

Key Action Steps for Phase 1

- Build the emotional bank account (with rounding and thank-you notes).

- Start to hardwire key behaviors.

- Reward and recognize.

- Introduce a new accountability system.

- Roll out behavior standards.

In this phase, it is important to build the emotional bank account through leader rounding and **Employee Thank You Notes** (tools described in chapter 11). Identify what the employees need: whether it is more communication or more structured reward and recognition. Then deliver it—especially quick wins like basic tools and equipment that people have needed, information about the organization that has not been shared in the past, and increased reward and recognition. Remove any existing or perceived barriers to work and ensure that staff have the basic supplies and equipment to do their jobs well. Make sure senior leaders are accessible and are seen as role modeling the right behaviors.

This is also the time when you start to hardwire key behaviors. By hardwiring, I mean that you build actions into the schedule and use a performance evaluation tool that aligns with the Pillar objectives and implementation of tools. This ensures that key actions get done. It's not optional.

An example of hardwiring rounding: Instead of suggesting that leaders round, ask nurse managers to develop a system so that nursing staff round for outcomes on X number of patients each day and report on identified issues for follow-up in a report.

Introduce the new leader evaluation tool and develop a timeline for making it operational within the next several months. This is also the time you want to roll out the standards of behavior, because excitement is high.

PHASE 2: Reality Sets In

What to Expect

- We/they

- Inconsistency

- Bigger than I thought

- This will impact me

- Some are getting it. Some are not.

In Phase 2, we start to see some of the "we/they" mentality and often hear "It's not our fault." There are inconsistencies.

Some departments might be doing peer interviewing while some aren't. Some leaders are buying in and some aren't. You begin to see the low performer, middle performer, and high performer spread out, and the inconsistencies become more apparent. This phase is important, because it shows that an organization is moving forward. But gaps between leaders and department performance start to become more apparent. This is a natural occurrence, even if we have good systems to hardwire key behaviors, because leaders are at different levels of performance.

The executive team, about this time, might begin to panic, thinking, "This is bigger than we thought!" That's why, like the runner training for the marathon, the executive team needs to learn about The Wall, which organizations hit in Phase 3.

Key Action Steps in Phase 2

- Elevate and focus training.

- Re-recruit high performers.

- Increase substance of communication to staff.

- Continue to implement hardwiring.

- Complete conversations with high, middle, and low performers (explained below).

During this phase, it is important to elevate and focus on training. For example, about this time, it becomes evident that there are some real success stories. So, ask the question, "What are they doing that would help others who aren't as successful?" In other words, what is it that makes them successful? Look at their skill sets and what systems they have hardwired. Share these with others. But we also want to do more than share their best practices. We need to re-recruit the middle and high performers and profile them. The speed of change in an organization is pegged to these leaders. We have to keep them moving.

PHASE 3: The Uncomfortable Gap

What to Expect

- **The Wall Appears** as the gap widens.
  More leaders and employees are really getting it.
  Some obviously are not until it becomes intolerable.

- Tougher decisions must be made.

- Process improvement increases.

- Need for standardization becomes evident.

- Inconsistencies become more obvious.

In Phase 3, there will be continued signs of progress. In fact, this may create a false sense of security. Why? Process improvement becomes evident about this time, because there are clear specific goals and a more mature team. A majority of the organization's performance has improved. Results across all Pillars are evident. People are now connected because they know this commitment to excellence is making their lives better.

You are also getting better feedback from your physicians and employees. Physicians will say, "I don't know what it is, but something's different around here." The labs are running better. Nurses seem better prepared because the organization has put systems and processes in place that are important to them. You'll hear three main things from employees: (1) Our leaders seem more visible; (2) Things we've been requesting for a while now are starting to appear (e.g., more blood pressure cuffs, IV monitors); and (3)Some of the problem people don't work here anymore.

But in Phase 3, the gap between the high/middle performers and low performers widens, and it widens to the point that the high and middle performers see the gap as unfair and not consistent with the values of the organization. Organizational performance will begin to stall. Ultimately, that spinning Flywheel slows to a stop. It is then that we have hit The Wall.

THE GAP IS INTOLERABLE

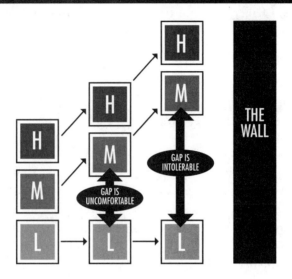

How Did This Happen?

Due to the growing gap between high, middle, and low performers, the high performers have done one of three things:

1. They have exited the organization. High performers cannot tolerate being part of an organization that won't perform. This exit is guaranteed if such an individual reports to a low performer. We have all heard of a high performing RN who chooses to leave rather than risking losing her licensure by working with low performers.

2. If for personal reasons they cannot exit, the high performer will find a way to fulfill this desire to learn, grow, and contribute outside of the organization, perhaps channeling these energies into leadership positions in professional membership organizations or by pursuing advanced degrees.

3. Or, they will still seem like a high performer, but will slow down and pace themselves, because they are frustrated with the organization. In summary, performance slows or drops.

The middle performers will just slow down, which will stall organizational performance.

The low performers are well rested. They knew they would outlast this initiative like all the others.

And once an organization has hit The Wall, it begins to look for new approaches to the same old problems, thinking its efforts must have been misdirected. We try on for size the Next Great Initiative we read about in a magazine. But we will only be disappointed. To create and sustain excellence, the core focus must always be on the Five Pillars of People, Quality, Service, Finance, and Growth.

Key Action Steps for Phase 3

- Elevate and focus training.

- Continue to re-recruit high performers.

- Increase substance of communication to staff.

- Finalize hardwiring.

- Promote your winners.

- Ensure that the "right people" are in the "right places."

Our first priority is to move the high and middle performers to a higher level of performance. This must be done first. Second, we must move the low performers up to a higher level of performance or out of the organization within a specific time frame. By doing so, we can move the high, middle, and low performers over The Wall and eliminate the anchor weighing down the organization. I will explain how to move high, middle, and low performers in greater detail in the next section.

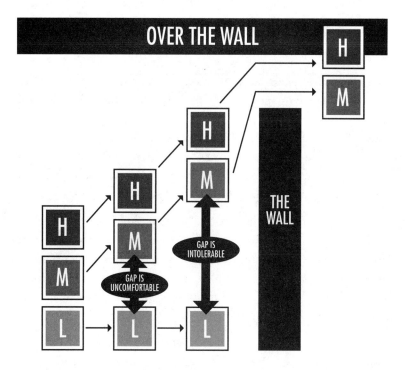

We also need to finalize hardwiring of key behaviors to reduce inconsistency in performance and make expectations clear. For example, by now, rounding on patients should be consistently hardwired across leadership with little variation in performance. Meeting deadlines becomes an important way to send a message about the organization's expectations of leaders. Conversations are more mature. In Phase 3, it's important to maintain focus on specific outcomes and results as described in the leadership evaluation tool.

PHASE 4: Consistency

What to Expect

- System-wide high-performing results

- Right leaders are in place

- Everyone understands the keys to success

- Disciplined people and disciplined processes

- Proactive leadership

In this phase, the organization has moved over The Wall because we have systematically addressed the high, middle, and low performers, and progress is continuing. As a result, we have a team of **disciplined leaders** in place. During this phase, there is going to be more proactive leadership. Leaders aren't going to wait for their superiors to come to them. Instead, they're going to see the problems and suggest solutions.

For example, if a leader sees that she isn't going to hit the budget in her department, she has two options. She can wait until the report comes out and somebody knocks on her door to talk about it, or she can go to her boss and say, "I've been tracking my expenses, and I'm going to be over budget. Let me tell you what I'm doing to get it back in line."

That's a huge difference from waiting for somebody else to ask you about it. We're talking about proactive leadership, which creates a self-motivated culture of excellence and high employee retention. The organization knows they have the right leaders in place, and they all understand the keys to success.

It's time to raise the bar for goals. And there's a clear understanding of cause and effect. Leaders understand that there are more variables to a decision than those that first meet the eye. And these actions create a result. For example, what if the hospital is in some financial trouble? Someone says, "We can save $22,000 by not having the employee picnic this year."

The next thing you know, as soon as you've canceled the picnic, your employee turnover has gone through the roof and you wonder what happened. It's because there was a cause and result from removing the employee picnic. Initially, you just saw the opportunity for a $22,000 savings. But to the employees, you removed a thank-you, a tradition, and a perk that their families had come to look forward to. They saw it as a huge slap in the face. They were never asked. They were only informed after the decision had been made. That's when several employees decided that they would rather go work where they were appreciated.

In 1995, the year before I arrived at Baptist Hospital, Inc., the organization had a difficult year financially. Every year for many years, each employee was given a $15 certificate to purchase a holiday turkey. But that year, they reduced the certificate to $12. Now, to the employees, the turkey certificate was sacred ground! They will never forget that incident for the rest of their lives. They will take that memory to their deathbeds. They called it "Turkeygate." Mature leaders in Phase 4 will have a greater sense of cause and effect and will be able to navigate difficult decisions more effectively.

Key Action Steps in Phase 4

- Push for innovation.

- Standardize and repeat key behaviors.

Stick to the path that got the organization to where it is, but take those actions to the next level. Recognize the proactive, self-confident leadership that has developed and realize that even in a well-run organization, challenges from the external environment (e.g., a larger than anticipated cut in reimbursement, a new physician-owned outpatient center) will create the need for even greater efficiency. But, because you have the right leaders in the right places, you can navigate these bumps in the road. You are building leadership competencies to adjust to a constantly changing environment. Also, look to all benchmarks across all Pillars. Because you have a mature leadership team, you can move beyond a focus only on internal improvement and use your benchmark data to drive towards becoming the best in class organization. Innovation becomes the key in Phase 4. In other words, how do we continually get better?

PHASE 5: Leading the Way — Results

What to Expect

- Employees have purpose.

- Patients choose your facility over others.

- Physicians want to work at your facility.

- We are changing health care for the better.

- What seemed to have been impossible is being achieved.

When you have passed Phase 4 in the organizational change process, you have succeeded at hardwiring excellence at the core of your organization's culture. The results show across all the Pillars, from more revenues, to lower employee turnover, to higher patient satisfaction.

This discussion about the five phases of organizational change is designed to help you anticipate the need for developing your leaders by giving them the skill set they will need to move through each phase. Of particular importance is a keen awareness about The Wall, for that is the reason that so many initiatives have failed in the past. We need to know when we are at risk of hitting The Wall and how to move over and forward. This is so important that I'd like to share insights into effective ways of communicating with high, medium, and low performers. This is a key step in overcoming The Wall.

HOW TO MOVE OPERATIONAL PERFORMANCE

As discussed in Phases 2 and 3, the reason for hitting The Wall is the gap between the high/middle performers and the low performers. It is like an anchor holding back the organization. The high and middle performers are frustrated because they feel they don't work for a fair leader. Some managers believe that if they treat all their employees the same they will be viewed as being fair. The truth is that if you treat the high, middle, and low performers the same, you will be less effective and may be viewed as unfair.

In fact, recently, I heard about a health care leader who said his biggest regret when looking back over his career was that he spent too much of his time with the low performers and not enough with the high performers.

Think for a minute of the bosses you have known. Can you think of one who did not deal with an employee whom you and others considered a low performer? What about the boss who kept that employee in the department for years? The boss may even have rated them as "meets expectations" on performance evaluations. What goes through your mind as you consider this individual's boss? Do you classify that boss as fair? What is your impression about their integrity and values? When I ask leaders if they are fair, 100 percent of hands go up. When I ask leaders if they have lower performers, most of the same hands go up. While we as leaders may see "fairness" and "dealing with low performers" as two separate issues, our staff clearly do not.

The High-Middle-Low Conversations

The high-middle-low conversations are a series of dialogues that a supervisor has with employees based on their performance rating. To complete this exercise there are four steps:

1. Place your employees in high, middle, or low category.

2. Meet with the high performers first.

3. Meet with the middle performers second.

4. Meet with the low performers last.

At Studer Group, we recommend that all leaders in the organization go through these four steps, beginning with senior leadership.

Step 1

Assessing your staff will help you recognize the high performers and middle performers so you can re-recruit your best workers and reward their efforts.

The first step is for leaders to make a list of all of their direct reports. Then rank them as high, middle, or low performers.

Step 2

Next, meet with the high performers and have a "retention" conversation.

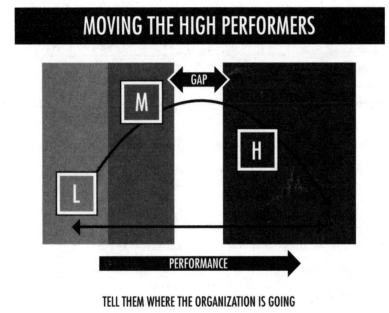

MOVING THE HIGH PERFORMERS

TELL THEM WHERE THE ORGANIZATION IS GOING

THANK THEM FOR THEIR WORK

OUTLINE WHY THEY ARE SO IMPORTANT

ASK IS THERE ANYTHING YOU CAN DO FOR THEM

High performers share the organization's values, are proactive, and suggest changes for process improvement. They are open to new ideas from anywhere within the organization and have the ability to get the job done. High performers have a positive attitude and are good role models and mentors to new employees.

The key message for high performers is to re-recruit them. Say, "I value you. I do not want you to leave. Is there anything that might cause you to think about leaving? What can I do to help you and your departments achieve your goals?"

We start with the high performers to build their confidence and skill in this process, but mostly to build an emotional bank account and set of supporters within the department. Word will get out very quickly that these conversations are occurring.

The CEO spends 15 to 30 minutes with each direct report, beginning with the person who role models the best leadership skills, obtains the best results, and contributes the most to the organization. Then the senior leadership team does the same thing with their direct reports. The directors do the same thing with their direct reports, and the managers then complete this same exercise with each of their front-line employees.

Step 3

The next step is to meet with your middle performers. The middle performers are good, solid employees. They can make or break an organization. They actively support the leaders in the organization and will let leadership know if there is a problem. The goal is to help them become high performers.

We need to invest in developing these employees and help them become high performers.

When meeting with your middle performers, inform them early that you want to retain them as an employee. We recommend a four-step process:

Reassure

Start with a supporting statement. Reassure the employee. Let them know they are valued.

Support

Tell them why they are important to the organization. Be specific.

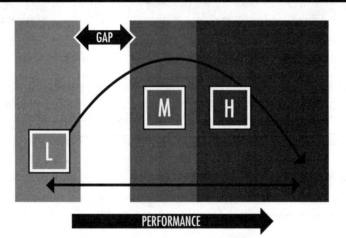

MOVING THE MIDDLE PERFORMERS

REASSURE INDIVIDUAL GOAL IS TO RETAIN:

S: SUPPORT - DESCRIBE GOOD QUALITIES

C: COACH - COVER DEVELOPMENT OPPORTUNTY

S: SUPPORT - REAFFIRM GOOD QUALITIES

Coach

Then coach the middle performer by sharing one area for development and improvement. Let them know that you have a concern, but share only one area.

Support

Finally, end the meeting with a support statement. Let them know that you are committed to their success. Ask if there is anything that you can do to help them in the area you just identified.

High performers will continue to move up. Most of the middle performers will also move up. The low performer is likely to remain where they are. At that time, the low performer will make a desperate bid to pull the middle performer back down.

Step 4

Finally, meet with the low performers.

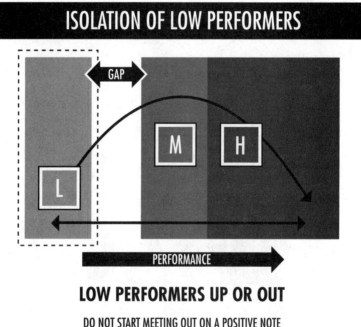

ISOLATION OF LOW PERFORMERS

LOW PERFORMERS UP OR OUT

DO NOT START MEETING OUT ON A POSITIVE NOTE

D: DESCRIBE - DESCRIBE WHAT HAS BEEN OBSERVED

E: EVALUATE - EVALUATE HOW YOU FEEL

S: SHOW - SHOW WHAT NEEDS TO BE DONE

K: KNOW - KNOW CONSEQUENCES OF CONTINUED SAME PERFORMANCE

While the high and middle performers are assets to the organization, the low performers negatively impact the organization as well as patient and employee satisfaction. If you have a low performer in the organization, it is likely they have little desire to grow or take on additional responsibilities beyond their current job. In addition, they may procrastinate, miss deadlines, and will not live by the organization's values. Low performers may have a negative attitude and take up a lot of management's time. False performance evaluations mislead employees and make termination more difficult for the employee and the managers. Addressing the low performer is difficult. When meeting with a low performer we recommend you follow the D-E-S-K approach.

You don't want to reward and recognize low performers. Do not start the meeting on a positive note or a compliment.

Describe

Begin the meeting by describing (D) the behavior you have seen. For example, "Lisa, you know one of the things I have noticed is that when you leave your work area, you often leave it in an inappropriate manner. Your coworkers who come in after you have a difficult time, because they've got to clean up what you've left." I have described what I've seen.

Evaluate

Second, evaluate (E) how you feel. "Lisa, I'm very disappointed that just 30 days ago when we met, you told me that this wouldn't happen again and you would fix it."

Show

Third, you want to show (S). "Lisa, at the end of your shift today, I'm going to come and show you exactly how the work area needs to look every time you leave."

Know

Finally, know (K) the consequences. "Lisa, you need to know the consequences. Right now this is a verbal warning, but if it happens again it will be a written warning. And if it happens after that it, it will mean termination. You need to know the consequences if you continue this behavior."

If the low performer is not dealt with, the high performers and middle performers become emotionally drained. They feel they are carrying people and start thinking leadership isn't fair. Again The Wall starts to form. One of the things that you will find in this journey is that if you have the right evaluation tool, the right leadership training, and you define the culture through the standards of behavior, the low performers become very obvious.

The reason these high, middle, and low performance conversations don't happen is not so much that the employee is so challenging, but that we have not trained middle managers how to have the conversations in the first place. We have to train them how, when, and with whom to have these conversations. That is why I believe an organization must develop a way to hardwire leadership training. We recommend that organizations sponsor their own Leadership Development Institutes (LDIs) quarterly.

LEADERSHIP DEVELOPMENT SESSIONS BUILD LEADERSHIP COMPETENCIES

To build the skill set of leadership, we recommend many things. One key recommendation is to take leaders off-site for two days every 90 days to participate in an LDI. By doing so, we ensure that we are hardwiring 64 hours of training every year (in contrast to an average of 6.5 hours of training annually in health care). The purpose of a Leadership Development Institute is to develop leaders' skills to enable the achievement of organizational goals, as well as to improve individual leadership performance and organizational consistency.

The 90-day period between LDI sessions allows for the feedback, coaching, and practice the leaders need to integrate the new skills into their daily practice.

Getting managers off-site is tremendously valuable. Leaders need an opportunity to get away from the noise and the tasks. Sometimes I think that if we just put everybody in a room for a day, we will walk out a better team just because we know each other a little bit better.

As I described earlier, leaders sometimes tell me that they can't do off-site training because they can't be gone that long from the department every 90 days. The ironic thing is that leaders are already gone from the department two days out of seven every week. I used to get a charge out of the fact that there were about 70 of us leaders running around during the day. Then at night, we threw the keys to a shift supervisor and didn't give it a second thought. Those shift supervisors hold the organization together.

In fact, once an organization sets up a Leadership Development Institute, leaders who may have been skeptical see the enormous benefit of taking time to improve their leadership skills. Let me share what some leaders at one organization felt after having been on this path for over a year.

On Attending LDIs

Since we've begun having the two-day leadership retreats, I've learned that we are all in the same boat. We are all working toward the same goals. This may sound stupid, because a health care organization should always be "working toward the same goals," but we were all trying to reach those goals in our own separate and individual ways. Now we are all doing the same thing the same way, and at last the left hand always knows what the right hand is doing. We have become a much better organized and cohesive group. The opportunity to share ideas and concerns with all of the leadership group at one time has been priceless. I am very proud to be part of an organization whose senior leadership is committed to excellence and expresses this commitment with associates at all levels. Common sense is making a strong comeback here!

Kim
Med/Surge Nurse Manager

Another Letter on the Benefits of LDIs

At my first retreat, I was overwhelmed. I thought, "They are crazy! We will never get all of this done!" But I listened intently because the principles seemed to make sense. So by the end of the retreat, I decided I would give it my all.

From then on, every Institute has gotten better. The employees that participate are wonderful and their talents have blossomed. Even so-called "average people" share their greatest knowledge and inspire others by their participation.

I want to retire, but I cannot leave this group of friends and fellow employees. Besides, I want to be there when we win the Baldrige award and finally have our new facility!

Determined to stay,

Linda
A leader

Setting Up a Leadership Development Institute

The goals under the Five Pillars guide the framework for establishing the objectives and the curriculum for each of the LDI sessions.

Let me give you an example. If reducing employee turnover is a goal under the People Pillar, then it is important to develop leader competencies for retaining employees. To achieve this goal, many types of training needs may be identified, including how to:

- Understand health care finance

- Maintain capacity management

- Conduct high, middle, and low performer conversations

- Round on staff

- Manage up

- Peer interview

- Hardwire thank you notes

- Use exit interviews to identify trends for improvement

- Roll out employee survey results and develop action plans

- Answer tough questions from staff

By providing this training at the LDI, leaders will develop concrete skills to achieve organizational goals.

Because curriculum needs to be tied to organizational goals, the CEO should be an active participant in the development and the on-going activities of the Institute. The CEO must articulate the vision and expected outcomes for the LDI, and review and approve the objectives, curriculum, and "Leaders Accountability Grid" with the senior leaders. The CEO will also provide an update on results by Pillar at the beginning of each session.

Who Runs the LDI

The LDI is led by a leader who is responsible for overall coordination of the LDI. This individual is typically a manager in the organization who agrees to take on this additional responsibility. Responsibilities of the LDI team leader can include: facilitating agenda-setting with the CEO and senior leaders, leading team meetings, managing budgets, and working with individual LDI team leaders. This person is also responsible for reporting results and giving updates to senior leadership.

Senior leaders demonstrate their commitment to the goals of the organization by actively participating in all sessions, modeling the behaviors they want the organization to adopt, and holding their leaders accountable for attendance at all leadership development sessions and behaviors identified in the leaders accountability grid.

The Leadership Development Institute is generally designed, developed, and implemented by teams of middle managers. (The members of the team are voted on by other middle managers.) It is important that leaders are designing their own training so it is relevant, practical, and focused on outcomes. These teams create the curriculum (based on the outcomes identified by senior leaders), manage the communication to attendees and the organization, select the venue, make sure all equipment is in place, and develop actions for the leaders accountability grid. The LDI teams we suggest are:

CURRICULUM

This team is responsible for designing what is taught at each training session. Their main focus is to fulfill the learning objectives set forth by the senior leadership. Sample curriculum topics could include: how to understand health care finance, how to maximize staff scheduling benefits, how to run an effective meeting, how to deliver negative news, or perhaps how to address a specific challenge the organization faces. The key is to do real work at these two-day sessions that you utilize immediately. So instead of reviewing an organizational case study, use your own organization and its data in any case study you present.

COMMUNICATION

The Communication Team provides key and pertinent information to leaders, employees, and physicians about the LDI. These individuals are responsible for keeping everyone informed of events and outcomes from leader learning and actions taken. They will communicate to leaders about their homework for the LDI and what will be taking place there, and also sharing with medical staff and employees what leaders will be learning at the LDI and what employees should look for when they return. For example, they might say, "At the LDI, your leaders will be learning about peer interviewing and will present how this works at your next department meeting."

SOCIAL

This team is responsible for setting the theme for each session, developing skits or role-playing activities, providing decorations, and creating other fun activities for leaders to participate in. A celebratory atmosphere fosters relationship-building and a more cohesive team. For instance, recently at one health care facility, 500 hospital leaders came together at an LDI and enjoyed watching the senior leadership team—led by the system president/CEO—do "The Leadership Shuffle," a spin-off on the well-loved Super Bowl Shuffle that Chicago Bears fans will remember from the mid 1980s. These activities break down barriers.

LOGISTICS

This team is responsible for providing the "nuts and bolts" of each session, including securing facilities for the training sessions and coordinating the provision of food and beverages, audio/visual equipment, and room set-up.

ACCOUNTABILITY

This team captures key learnings at training sessions for continued use by leaders, further organizational dissemination, or ongoing learning. The team turns learnings into specific assignments or behaviors that will be implemented in the next 90 days and identifies anticipated results to review at the next LDI that are based on reports about these actions. Early on, an organization might use an Accountability Grid, which is basically an assignment sheet about actions to be completed. However, once an organization has implemented 90-day work plans, the Accountability Grid is no longer needed. (The assignments are integrated into individual work plans.)

The structure of all of the teams can be modified, depending on the size of the leadership group or organization.

In the cases of health care systems, each LDI team (i.e., Logistics, Curriculum, etc.) may include a representative from each hospital. The key is to develop the structure that is appropriate to the organization and ensures that all LDI responsibilities are assigned.

In summary, a Leadership Development Institute provides the tools and training leaders need to achieve the goals of the organization and facilitates the process of connecting those results to purpose, worthwhile work, and making a difference.

I would like to share a final letter that a leader shared with me . . .

WHAT IT MEANS TO AN EMPLOYEE

My organization's commitment to training demonstrates to me how valuable I am as a person and as a resource to the organization. It affirms that senior leadership has confidence in my abilities to achieve and produce meaningful outcomes. That in return bolsters my self-esteem and re-affirms my commitment back to the success of the organization.

A year and half since the beginning of this journey, I now know that I can succeed...that I can contribute to successful outcomes, and that I can make a positive difference in the stressful world of health care for my patients, my organization, and my associates. While I still have 80-plus employees that report to me, my stress level has been reduced by at least half of what it was just 18 months ago. And for this I'm thankful.

Tim
Nurse Manager, Tennessee Hospital

If the greatest percentage of employees leave their jobs because of their relationship with their supervisor, then the best thing that we can offer an employee and an organization is a great leader.

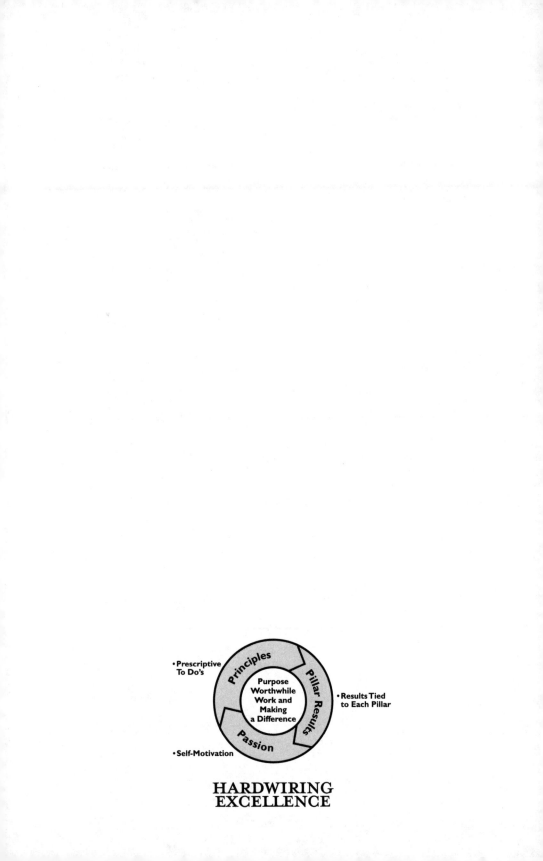

• Prescriptive
  To Do's

Principles

Pillar Results

Purpose
Worthwhile
Work and
Making
a Difference

• Results Tied
  to Each Pillar

Passion

• Self-Motivation

HARDWIRING
EXCELLENCE

CHAPTER SEVEN

PRINCIPLE 5
FOCUS ON EMPLOYEE SATISFACTION

Satisfied employees do a better job. It's just that simple. Principle 5 shows how an organization can drive operational results by focusing on employee satisfaction.

Do you remember the story of George Bailey in the movie *It's a Wonderful Life?* He was going to end his life as he faced the shame of bankruptcy with the police hot on his trail. He believed his whole life had been a waste. He wanted to get out of Bedford Falls, but events just kept conspiring to keep him there. He got stuck working at a Building and Loan that he didn't like. He got stuck in a house he wasn't that happy with. And he wasn't too thrilled with his wife Mary and the kids.

"Hee Haw"—the man Mary could have married—got out of Bedford Falls. He made big money in New York. Brother Harry was a hero in the war. George tried to serve his country but flunked his physical since he couldn't hear in one ear— because years before, he had jumped into the icy water to save his kid brother Harry from drowning.

So George goes to the bridge to end his life, but he ends up jumping in to save Clarence, his guardian angel. (Clarence had been sent down to earn his wings by helping George, for George was discouraged.) And then it happens—Clarence takes George back through his own life to show him what Bedford Falls would have been like without his life of service. How the low-income families would have suffered without the opportunity to buy homes through the Building and Loan that George ran. How his wife never would have married and his children never would have been born. George is overwhelmed at the vision of what might not have been—and the important ways he has touched so many in the town.

Near the end of the movie, George runs through town, yelling, "I love you, Bedford Falls!" Potter, the miserly banker, sees him and mutters, "Go home, George Bailey, because they're going to arrest you!" So George goes back into his house (which he has always hated because it's old, drafty, and they can't afford the repairs). He picks up that thing on the stairs that falls off all the time. But instead of slamming it down as usual, he pats it. He now loves the kids who were driving him nuts with their singing and piano-playing a little while ago. Mary shows up beaming with surprise, and he hugs her and tells her he loves her. All of a sudden, the whole town shows up. People of all colors, vocations, and backgrounds.

The people give George a basket full of money that they have all scraped together to help George out of his financial crisis. Hee Haw sends a telegram that he's sending $25,000. The police rip up the warrant for his arrest. Then his brother Harry shows up. He has just returned from the war and flown through a snowstorm to be with his brother George. He says, "I want to toast my brother George—the richest man in the world!" And, of course, as the tinkling bell indicates, Clarence gets his wings.

What changed in those two hours?

Had the town changed? Had the Building and Loan changed?

Had Mary changed?

Did the house change?

Did the kids change?

Did Potter change?

What changed was George.

Why?

Because somebody showed him purpose, worthwhile work, and making a difference.

What we did at Holy Cross was to show a little bit of that movie. Then we asked every department manager to write a script, "If Our Department Didn't Exist, What Would Happen to Our Organization?" We wanted everybody in that hospital to know that they had purpose, did worthwhile work, and were making a difference.

I think that with or without the movie, you could ask the employees at your hospital or department the same question.

Employees want three things:

1. *They want to believe the organization has the right purpose.* That's why the manager who makes himself look good at the expense of the senior leadership does a disservice to all the other employees. Because the senior leader represents "purpose" to the employees. And if employees don't feel good about the senior leaders, then they don't feel good about the organization. We can't have a "We/They" culture.

2. *They want to know that their job is worthwhile.* That's why they got into health care! They want you to know what they do is worthwhile work.

3. *They want to make a difference.* The results of what they do fuel their passion. So getting results remotivates people to persevere and seek more results.

I truly believe that leaders do all three of those things in health care. But I also think that what happens is that sometimes we forget to capture the positive "wins" because we have so much noise coming at us each day. And we have been trained to focus on what's wrong.

FOCUSING ON THE POSITIVE

To help us focus on the positive and ensure staff feels purpose, worthwhile work, and making a difference, here are three ideas to implement right away:

1. Harvest wins. In your administrative meetings, put this at the top of your agenda: "What wins have we achieved this week, and how are we communicating them throughout the system?" (You'll see this on the Agenda by Pillar tool I mentioned earlier.)

2. Add "rounding for positives" to your rounding skill set (detailed below).

3. Harvest and share examples where employees are making a difference. I will share more about how to do this in chapter 10 on "Communicate at All Levels."

THE #1 ACTION TO DRIVE EMPLOYEE
MUST HAVE ➤ SATISFACTION IS ROUNDING FOR OUTCOMES

While focusing on the positive is important, I believe that if there are only a few things you take away from this book, one should be **Rounding for Outcomes**. In fact, that is why it is a Must Have.

If you are like me, you'll probably say that you're already doing each of these Must Haves. I would have said so too, at one time. In fact, during that time, if people had asked me if I rounded, I would have said, "You bet! I can do the whole hospital in less than 30 minutes." In fact, I'd say to my assistant, "I'm going to go round. I'll be back in 18 minutes."

And I'd walk through the floors and flash a thumbs-up to employees as I passed by. I would ask people, "How you doing?" Usually they'd say, "Fine." I'd say, "Great!" and keep up my pace. If someone *should* say something like, "We're understaffed," I'd say, "Hang in there!" and move on.

Rounding for Outcomes is different than what I thought it was. Here's what I mean:

First, all leaders must round. Let me give you an example of effective rounding by a nurse leader or unit leader. As a nurse manager, I'm going to first round for the employee and not the patient. If I'm concentrating on employee satisfaction, employee retention, and physician loyalty, that will lay a strong foundation for higher patient satisfaction.

UNIT LEADER ROUNDING ON EMPLOYEES

As the nurse manager, the first thing I'm going to do is walk through the unit and build relationships. As leaders, we have a "to do" list, don't we? Leaders tend to be task-oriented. You have to get through your list or the reality is it will just keep growing.

But the staff wants a relationship with you. That is a legitimate need of theirs. (Remember, a poor relationship with the supervisor is the reason 39% of staff leave their jobs!) An RN is not going to go find another position, he's going to go find another hospital. So in reality, the most important thing you as a leader can do to not lose nurses is to build that relationship.

When leaders round, it is key for leaders to recognize the employees' needs. What are employees specifically looking for from their bosses or leaders?

- A good relationship

- Approachability

- Willingness to work side by side

- Efficient systems

- Training and development

- Tools and equipment to do the job

- Appreciation

That is why rounding is so powerful. It helps a leader meet these needs. Going back to my rounding example, if I am a nurse leader, I'm going to start by asking my staff questions to build our personal relationship (e.g., "How are your kids?" "Was it a great vacation?").

So if the first person I visit with is Sue on 11B, I might ask her about how her daughter's first day of school went. How her mom's doing. If she got her car out of the shop. I'm relationship-building.

It's important always to start with a personal question. Then I'm going to get more specific with my questions to drill down on the needs above. The five remaining questions we recommend in **Rounding for Outcomes** are:

- Tell me what is working well today?

- Are there any individuals whom I should be recognizing?

- Are there any physicians whom I should be recognizing? (if you are in an area with physician interaction)

- Is there anything we can do better?

- Do you have the tools and equipment to do your job?

When I consistently ask, **"Sue, tell me what's working well today?"** she will switch her focus from the negative to the positive. When it comes to patients, they count on us to be diagnosing problems. We're trained to look at what's wrong. But we also need to train ourselves to look at what's right.

As I said before, it's unusual for Plant Operations to get a call about how great the temperature is. When is the last time the lab got a call from a nurse saying, "Thanks for getting those lab reports up here on time. Bless you"?

When *does* the lab hear from the nurses? When things go wrong. And then we wonder why they have some negative feelings. By asking about what's going well, I can change the flow of thinking and conversation.

Sue might say, "Well, the meals went smoothly. And we got our lab reports right on time."

I say, "Thanks, Sue. I know Food Services and the lab are working hard. They will appreciate the kind words."

I can now harvest those two wins. I can call or stop by Food Services and the lab and say, "I was on the unit a few minutes ago, and they were quite complimentary of you for being on time."

That spreads through Food Services and the lab like wild fire. How do you think the service will be the next day? Even better. I'm harvesting wins and bringing them back to the departments. That positive feedback helps reward and recognize desired behavior. Recognized behavior gets repeated. I call this cycle *Success Builds Success*.

Now let's connect the dots. That is, let's understand the value of harvesting wins while rounding. Why is this type of exercise good for the patients? Because it increases their quality of care and improves service.

In reality, we're trying to re-recruit our staff all the time. Here's one reason this is important: I often ask RNs, "When was the last time a search firm or an agency called to try to get you to quit and come work for them?"

The answer is usually less than a week, and often *less than 24 hours!*

"Did you get the call at work or at home?"

"At work," they say.

"How about before that last call, when else did you get called?"

It's always less than a week.

Recognize that fact. Your staff is being recruited all the time by recruitment firms, agencies, and other health care providers. They even use *your* fax machines!

We senior executives act like that's how much in demand we are, too. But the average CEO position in health care gets about 300 applicants. And then it's a lengthy selection process.

When your competitors call your nurses, guess when they ask them to start?

Tomorrow.

If you're not on the field, constantly recruiting staff, you'll lose them.

While I'm on the floor, I'm also going to ask Sue, **"Are there any individuals I should be rewarding and recognizing today?"**

And Sue may tell me about Chuck, a housekeeper who went out of his way to be helpful this morning. So, I'm going to find Chuck and tell him that I was talking to Sue this morning, and she was very complimentary of how helpful he was.

How do you think Chuck will feel about Sue and the rest of the staff on 11B? What have I just done for coworker relationships?

Next, I'm going to ask, *"Are there any physicians I should be recognizing today?"* I ask this question because physicians do great things daily and they don't get rewarded and recognized very often. When do we notice the physician? When something goes wrong.

So Sue says, "Dr. Ruby really had a difficult surgery this morning, but he was really great with the family. In fact, he's down in the patient's room right now."

I can then go down and see Dr. Ruby and say, "Dr. Ruby, I was talking to Sue, a nurse on 11B, and she was telling me of the challenging surgery you had this morning and how wonderfully you worked with the family. Thank you for what you did. It's physicians like you who make this a great hospital."

How do you think the doctor feels? How do you think he feels about the nursing staff? We're building an emotional bank account with him.

Again, if you'll notice, I've been describing **Rounding for Outcomes,** and I've not gotten to the patient yet. I think the number one person we round on is the employee. And if we skip the employee, we're making a mistake. That is why **Rounding for Outcomes** fits within our discussion of Principle 5, "Employee Satisfaction."

Then I'll ask Sue, **"Is there anything we can do better?"** Even though I want the positive, I also want to capture ways to increase efficiency. If the system is broken, I need to know about it and fix it. It's called "process improvement."

I will also ask, **"Do you have the tools and equipment you need to do your job?"**

As I mentioned, at Holy Cross Hospital, when we first started rounding and went to a nursing unit, I asked the nurses if they had the tools and equipment they needed. They said, "We need a copy machine."

We made a decision in Administration to get copy machines for each nursing unit. And we decided to get rid of the key.

One thing I've learned is that when you're making a change, it sometimes helps to find something symbolic that impacts a lot of people to show you're listening. Getting rid of the copy machine keys impacted every department in the hospital. I also learned that visuals have a big impact. At the time we happened to be doing some construction at the hospital and there was a piece of equipment on-site that smashed black top. So, we sent out a flyer to all employees saying that we were going to smash the copy keys at two o'clock in the afternoon out on the blacktop.

At 2:00, we had the keys in a big pile in the parking lot and since Holy Cross was a Catholic Hospital, we loaded Sister Juline, one of the sisters of Saint Casimir, on the machine. This is where I learned another valuable lesson: Before putting a sister on a piece of large, heavy equipment, find out if she's ever driven a car! After a few jolts from the clutch and securely resituating her habit, Sister Juline charged forward and smashed the keys.

It was great fun for all of us there in the parking lot. Afterwards, I had a clear understanding of the impact of the visual display of change. All of a sudden, we heard cheering. When we turned around to the hospital, many of the employees who couldn't come out to the parking lot had actually walked over to the windows and were cheering! This wasn't about getting rid of keys. It was about creating more trust in the organization. And it started with a simple question during rounding.

Never underestimate the difference that simple changes and decisions can make in the eyes of the physicians, the employees, and the patients.

Unit Leader Rounding on Patients

Once I have focused on the employees, I can then redirect my focus to the patients. Before doing so, I am going to say to Sue, **"I'm going to be rounding on patients. Is there anything I need to know before I go into the patients' rooms?"** I want to be prepared. It looks like pretty bad teamwork if the nurse manager doesn't know about a patient's situation. If the patient has suffered terrible news, for example, I need to know about it ahead of time.

Then I'm going to enter the patient's room. As I do, I will say something like, "Hi, Mrs. Hall, I'm Quint Studer. I'm the nurse manager here on 11B. Let me give you my card with my phone number on it. We want to make sure while you're here that you're very satisfied with our care. If there's anything that we can do to make sure that you're very satisfied, let us know."

I'll also see the name of the nurse written on the white board in the room, so I'll say, "Oh, I see Debbie is your nurse. She's excellent. She'll take great care of you. You'll really like her. And I see Dr. Ruby is your physician. He's one of the best in his field." Through rounding, I'm managing up.

TIP: *Consider beginning meetings only after 10 a.m. with the firm understanding that the time before 10 a.m. is spent rounding in work areas.*

Rounding for Outcomes doesn't have to take long. That's because it's focused. If I'm the orthopedic nurse manager speaking with a patient who has had a total knee replacement, I'm going to talk about pain management, because I know they don't care about food or housekeeping. They care about pain! If I'm the OB nurse manager, I know the patients are already worried about going home, so I'm going to ask about any concerns or questions they have about taking care of the baby at home. In other words, I'm going to round based on their needs and concerns.

But I also want to dig deeper.

So, I'll also ask, **"Is there anybody on the staff who has really done a nice job for you?"**

Mrs. Hall gives me the name of her nurse, Bob. Then I'm going to ask what Bob did to make her feel that way. I need a *specific* behavior to recognize because I want that behavior repeated and imitated by other staff members.

So if Mrs. Hall tells me that Bob took the time to go over her whole schedule with her, I'll later make a point of finding Bob and telling him that Mrs. Hall was very complimentary of him and appreciated his taking the time to go over the schedule with her. And I'll thank him for the good job. And if I happen to see the CNO later, I'll ask her to please say something to Bob about the good job he's been doing.

How do you think Bob will feel?

How do you think he'll feel about the hospital?

About his job?

About the administration?

About serving the patients?

How do you think he'll feel about taking the time to go over a patient's schedule the next time? He's going to do it again. **When we hear a patient say someone did a good job, we have to push for specifics, because we're creating a template to align the behaviors of all staff members to match Bob's behavior with Mrs. Hall.**

I'm going to leave the patient's room by once again saying something like, **"Is there anything I can do for you right now? I have time."**

We've learned that if you don't say that you have time, they'll assume you're too busy and won't ask. Except that they'll hit the call light later. When you say you have time, you can decrease call lights dramatically. In fact, one organization studied the effect of key words on call lights and determined that when someone says, "Is there anything else I can do? I have the time," patients are more likely to raise their questions before the nurse leaves the room, decreasing call lights by 40 percent.

That's **Rounding for Outcomes**. You've probably noticed that it serves many purposes. We accomplished some employee retention, staff building, reward and recognition, physician satisfaction, patient satisfaction, and process improvement. In fact, **Rounding for Outcomes** drives results across all Five Pillars.

This is one of the most important actions you can take to turn the Flywheel. It's a single approach with a multiple focus. And it's not easy, because at first you can be overwhelmed by the number of systems that haven't been fixed in a long time. Plus, you are busy identifying process improvement opportunities while also increasing the time you spend on reward and recognition. And while you're rounding, you are at times observing sub-par performers. So at first, rounding actually creates more work.

But once you've been at it for four to six months—once the processes have been improved, systems are working well, staff have the tools and equipment they need, physician issues have been addressed, and sub-par performers have been dealt with—rounding takes much less time and in fact becomes one of the most enjoyable aspects of a manager's job. They will tell you so!

Now, instead of rounding to react, we are able to round in a proactive way to look for additional process improvement. At Studer Group, we actually recommend that hospitals hardwire rounding reports because when we document what is working, we can fix systems, pass recognition to leaders, and identify issues that will help our employees be more efficient and effective, rather than just holding peoples' feet to the fire. One way to make sure rounding gets done is to use rounding logs that track frequency, outcomes, and follow-up from rounding. **We strongly recommend hardwiring Rounding for Outcomes by integrating it into daily operations.**

I have found that for many leaders, rounding is not a natural process. For those who do it naturally, good results are probably already happening.

On Harvesting Wins from Rounding

Once I was at a hospital when the CEO (also a physician) asked me to show him how I rounded when I was a hospital president. I was impressed. Here was a physician CEO who was continually looking for ways to improve his own skill set. So, as we exited the elevator and were about to enter a nursing unit, we noticed a woman reading a sign on the wall. Now, most of us would assess a person like this as "occupied" and walk by.

Instead, I walked up to her and asked, "May I help you?"

She said, "Do you work here?"

I said, "No, but he's the CEO," at which point the CEO introduced himself.

The woman said, "I've been wanting to talk to you. My mother has been in many hospitals and this is the best one she has ever been in."

Of course, I could see his sigh of relief as she said this with me standing there. He thanked her and was ready to keep walking.

But I said, "Tell me why you feel this hospital is so good? What do they do?"

"The nursing staff are just phenomenal," she explained. "They are so good at keeping the family informed."

I told her we were headed up to the unit and asked if she remembered any of their names. She apologized that she didn't.

So I said, "Before your mother leaves, would you write down their names and send them down to the CEO? He'll make sure they are recognized for their great service."

She said she would. So I then asked, "And how are your mother's physicians?"

She said they were excellent, so I asked the CEO to compliment them as well.

Finally, I said, "When your mother goes home, she'll be getting a survey in 10 to 14 days. Many times the family helps patients fill these out. This is how the hospital keeps track of how patients feel about their care. I'd really appreciate it if you'd fill it out when it comes and return it. And any names of staff that you include on there will be recognized."

After that, we walked to the unit and the CEO told the nurses about our great conversation. They felt wonderful and so appreciative of the daughter of the patient they were caring for. In fact, I imagine that when she next came in to see her mother, they expressed their appreciation for her compliment. And I also suspect that that patient's daughter was now looking for the names of staff she could recognize when the survey came. She was even more acutely aware of the excellent care her mother was receiving.

What if we had just walked past that woman? We would have missed the opportunity to collect names of nurses and physicians to recognize and convey an understanding of the importance of the survey.

After this experience, the CEO called all his leaders together and explained that in spite of all his years as a physician and leader, he'd only just recently learned what it really means to **Round for Outcomes**. As a result of that meeting, the leadership team committed to working the hallways aggressively for the next 90 days, **Rounding for Outcomes.**

Today that hospital has RN turnover below 10%, patient satisfaction above 95th percentile, and has won a prestigious statewide award for quality as well as Magnet status for nursing.

Different Types of Rounding for Outcomes

There are three types of rounding: (1) Unit Manager Rounding, (2) Senior Leader Rounding, and (3) Support Department Rounding on Other Departments. (You can read more at *www.studergroup.com* on how these differ and work together to operationalize excellence.) However, I urge you to begin by hardwiring Unit Manager Rounding, because that will have the most impact. It works in nursing, pharmacy, lab, medical offices, and human resources. It works for everyone. Rounding by the unit manager drives results. While employees might like the CEO, if they don't like the unit manager, we're done.

A Systematic Approach to Employee Satisfaction

There is another important tool—in addition to **Rounding for Outcomes**—that drives employee satisfaction and results across all Five Pillars. It is an organization-wide employee survey. The key to these surveys is not the data itself. The key is how well you share the data with the staff, and how you communicate action based on their feedback.

At Baptist Hospital, Inc., in February 1996, only 666 out of 1,700 people (39% of employees) filled in the first employee satisfaction survey. So this was the foundation for action when I arrived in 1996. The second time we did the survey in 1997, 80 percent of employees completed the survey. And in 1999, 94 percent filled it out. We never changed how we did the survey. What changed was employees' perceptions about the impact their opinions would have on changes we would make in the organization. After seeing results, more employees wanted to have input.

How to Use an Employee Survey Effectively

Many organizations already use an employee survey tool. That is fine. For organizations that don't, they can select one from many survey vendors or develop their own. It's the process after the survey is completed that is most important.

Once the survey is complete and data has been collected, Studer Group trains managers how to explain the results of the employee satisfaction survey. While survey vendors are excellent at helping an organization to interpret the data, it's also important to set leaders up for success as they communicate challenges and opportunities to employees. Our coaches recommend that the entire leadership team go off-site for a half day, roll out the survey results, and teach leaders how to develop key words and actions for the survey rollout meeting they will have with staff.

For example, if a manager got bad results, we'd urge him or her to share these results with staff by saying something like:

"The employee satisfaction results are back. Thank you for completing the survey. I want to tell you I'm disappointed. Obviously I'm not the leader that I want to be. But I want you to know that I'm committed to being a good leader. In fact, I'm going to get additional training in the areas you identified where I can improve. I do want to tell you that I'm committed to making this a better department and to being a good leader. I hope you'll help me."

Once you say, "I hope you'll help me," they're on your side.

A big part of employee satisfaction discussions is the ability to be open about the results. For example, the same manager, in a meeting with the department, might say:

"Here are the areas that you told me are the most important issues in this department, but I think some of you didn't fill out the survey, plus things could have changed. Let's read the five most important issues, based on the survey results. But I also want to give everybody a chance to add to this list. Sally, do you have anything to add? Nancy, do you have anything to add?"

So by the end of the meeting, you may have eight issues instead of just the top five from the survey. Ask everyone to vote on which one they believe is the biggest issue. This helps individuals to see that their priority might not be the same as everyone else's priority, even though they assumed it was.

After the vote, focus on the top three issues. Eventually, all of them will be addressed, but start with the top three. These could range from work pressure and communication issues to cleanliness or storage needs. There will be some quick wins sitting there that leaders can address easily to build that emotional bank account with staff. Then vote on some actions to take and assign responsibilities. Finally, the employees will fill out an evaluation form for the roll-out meeting itself. Let me explain why this evaluation form is important.

How the leader rolls out the employee survey can make or break the success of that tool. By asking employees to evaluate the roll-out meeting, you will accomplish three things:

1. Hardwire the roll-out process by holding the leaders accountable.

2. Provide employees an opportunity to share additional feedback about the process from which the leader can learn.

3. Monitor the success of the leader in the roll-out process so the leader's supervisor can provide additional coaching as needed.

At each session, the supervisor hands out an evaluation form on the roll out and asks employees to collect the completed forms, place them in a sealed envelope, and send them down to Administration. Then they are disseminated to the appropriate vice president who meets with the leader.

This evaluation process—how well the leader rolled out the results and developed an action plan with staff—is the missing element of most survey roll outs. It's essential that the leader's supervisor understand how well he or she communicated the results to staff.

We have found that about 95 percent of the time, when leaders have the proper training in using key words during our roll-out process, employees are already ranking the leader highly in how well they communicated results and offered opportunities for input. This boosts the leader's self-confidence as they continue to roll out survey results to more employees. This is but one example of leadership training that creates a more self-confident leader.

For the five percent of leaders whose staff feedback shows they are struggling to do this well, the supervisor can provide help immediately, before the next survey. Senior leaders also gain an opportunity to further review this individual's leadership skill set and ability. That's leadership coaching, development, and accountability.

EMPLOYEE SATISFACTION SURVEY DISCUSSION EVALUATION FORM

Please complete the following survey evaluation. All information will be anonymous and confidential.
We are sincerely interested in your opinion.
There will be absolutely no retribution for your candid responses.

Please answer the following questions by circling the number that best represents your opinion.

Supervisor: _____

	STRONGLY DISAGREE	DISAGREE	SOMEWHAT AGREE	AGREE	STRONGLY AGREE
My manager presented the employee satisfaction survey results in a complete and open manner.	1	2	3	4	5
I was given opportunity to provide feedback and voice my opinion	1	2	3	4	5
I agree with the priorities for action that my group came up with	1	2	3	4	5
I feel action will be taken by my manager	1	2	3	4	5
I feel action will be taken by my administration	1	2	3	4	5

Comments: _____
_____
_____
_____

Thank you for filling out this survey. Your response will be collected, and delivered to <name>.

NEXT STEPS

Once agreement about the top two or three opportunities for improvement has been reached with employees, they are placed on a written 90-Day Action Plan so they get addressed in the next quarter. Then the action plans are posted on the unit, with a copy sent to Administration. At the end of the 90 days, the leader sends a copy of the original plan with an update on progress to senior leaders.

We find that in a typical hospital, one issue per leader/department has been brought to closure. So in an organization with 100 leaders, you can expect 100 improvements for employee satisfaction as a result of that employee survey roll-out meeting. Of course the final step is for the CEO to communicate this accomplishment back to staff, by connecting the dots on how these achievements represent employee willingness to complete the survey initially, help prioritize their biggest concerns at the roll-out meeting, and take consistent action as identified in the 90-Day Action Plan.

SAMPLE NOTE FROM A CEO

To: All Employees

Based on your employee input, our meetings, and our hard work over the last 90 days, we've accomplished 111 things to make this a better place for patients, physicians, and employees. Here are a few examples . . .

Thank you.

So to sum up, I've shared three key actions to drive employee satisfaction and get results across all Pillars: (1) how to focus on the positives, (2) **Rounding for Outcomes,** and (3) effectively using an employee survey tool. The goal is to get a critical mass of employees on board as quickly as possible.

WHAT'S THE WHAT?

Leaders often ask me, "When do you get that critical mass of employees on board?"

It's such a great question. I like to explain that organizations will get more employees and physicians on board when they learn "What's the what." Then they can deliver "the what" or explain why they can't. It can be different for every person. For one, it might be finally an on-time evaluation. To another, it might be when a barrier is removed.

I'd like to share one of my favorite stories about the time I learned "what the what" was in a surgical intensive care nursing unit (SINU).

When I first got to Baptist, the administrative offices were on the fifth floor. Employees called these offices "The Penthouse." I eventually moved my office close to the cafeteria, but back then it was on the fifth floor. When making my way through the hospital, I had a habit of getting off the elevator and taking short cuts through departments so I could talk to staff. About once a week, when I got off the elevator, I would turn left and go through the SINU.

First, I'd go through the family waiting room and stop and speak to families to find out how they thought we were doing. Then I'd go into the unit and share compliments that I heard with staff. Next, I'd walk into at least one patient room with a family member, introduce myself and get to know them.

Inevitably, they would tell me about their loved one. Once, as a mother was telling me about her son with a serious brain injury who wanted to be a pilot, I noticed how much the nurse touched the boy and how much the family seemed to appreciate this and felt better about his care. The nurse would rub his cheek, comb his hair, or just put a hand on his shoulder. I noticed how most families seemed to like this.

Well I like results, and I like them fast. So I figured if a little extra touching would make a difference, I'd rub my body over the entire SINU if I had to.

One day, I came down the elevator, took a left into the SINU waiting room, talked to families and heard the now usual compliments about the staff. I then went into the unit and shared those compliments with the staff. Then—I don't know why exactly—I noticed four or five Mr. Coffee machines brewing hot water. And, since I was getting more comfortable with the staff, I thought I'd make some conversation.

So I said, "You guys must really like tea."

They looked at me with an expression of pure wonderment that clearly said, "Where does this guy come up with these things?" It was obvious we weren't connecting, so I motioned to the Mr. Coffees.

One of the nurses explained, "That's not for tea. It's for baths."

I figured it must be a temporary situation. Now, our hospital was built in 1951, and over the years, it had experienced multiple additions to increase capacity. So it couldn't be that they never had hot water, but I know there can be inconsistency at times.

I asked them, "How long have you had problems getting hot water?"

One of the nurses said, "Gee, I don't know. I've only been here 13 years."

Fifteen years ago, a nurse manager probably wrote a request to fix the hot water issue. For some reason, it couldn't be done. Then she likely did it again the next year. And once again, nothing happened. What do you think she did the third year? She didn't request it and figured out her own solution.

In fact, I was with a hospital COO not long ago, and he was up on a nursing unit. He saw a unit secretary use a four-hole punch and then take a single-hole punch to get the fifth hole. When he asked if it might not be easier to use a five-hole punch, the unit clerk said, "Absolutely, but we have been requesting one for awhile and just can't seem to get one." Sometimes tool and equipment needs are so obvious to employees, but leaders miss them as they appear to be little things, but they just aren't little to the staff.

In the case of the SINU nurses who needed hot water, I knew that no matter what I wrote in a newsletter or said in an Employee Forum, it wouldn't convince employees of my commitment to making the hospital a better place to work. I needed to show how I could help remove barriers in a tangible way.

So I talked to Plant Ops, who came up with the idea of putting heat pumps at each sink.

When Plant Ops told me that heat pumps were installed, I went back to SINU and asked staff, "How's the hot water?"

What do you think they did? They said, "Thank you." Being a man, I'd been sort of hoping they'd put my name on the refrigerator in recognition or something. But I did say, "Your managers have asked for this for awhile. I'm sorry we weren't more responsive." I didn't want to create that "we/they" dynamic by making myself look good at the expense of their managers.

So, then I went in to talk to a family in a patient's room. But just as I was leaving the unit, Maureen, an SINU nurse, came up to me and said, "Quint, can I talk to you?"

Now Maureen was focused and intense as she had to be with the seriousness of her patients' conditions. She was busy, and so cut straight to the chase.

She said, "You know, Quint. You come in here a lot."

I was quite relieved at the time because it seemed like it would be a positive conversation. She obviously had been noticing my efforts to be visible.

Then she said, "You do a lot of touching."

I started to relax even more because she was noticing my compassion.

At this time, I quickly thought back to a period during my early thirties when I struggled with receiving compliments. I had to make a prolonged and conscientious effort to stop "filtering out the positives." In those days, it was easier for me to focus on the negatives than on what was going right. And I think this happens to a lot of people in health care.

Anyway, since I was about to get a compliment, I was concentrating on graciously receiving it.

Then Maureen says, "We have infections in this unit."

Of course, I am caught off guard. How did we go from compliment to infection? And then she says, "And you don't wash your hands. You need to wash your hands."

Maureen points to the sinks throughout the unit, and then she turns and goes back to patient care. I'm still wondering where my compliment is. I later figured out that she was the spokesperson for the SINU staff. One of the co-workers probably said, "Who's going to tell him?" And another said, "You tell him, Maureen." When she came back, they probably gave her low fives.

So as I'm walking back down the hallway, I'm feeling a little nervous about all those infections I might have exposed myself to. How long have those infections been in this nursing unit? And when did the nurses notice I wasn't washing my hands?

When do you think? I bet the first day, the first patient.

How come it took them twelve weeks to tell me? Then it hit me. Until they got hot water, they didn't care whether I lived or died. I had become a commodity.

In fact, in health care, I believe we have taken the word "Administration," which derives from "administer" or "minister to," and made ourselves into a commodity. It seems that leaders come and go just like initiatives that come and go.

It all makes me think of Starbucks. Starbucks took a commodity—a coffee bean—and turned it into an experience. Have we achieved that with leaders in health care?

When I speak to groups of health care employees around the country, I often tease, "If I hooked up all of you to a monitor to measure positive reactions and showed you a picture of Administration followed by a picture of Starbucks, which would get a more positive reaction?"

Fortunately, today we are changing that. So my message is: You don't know "what the what" is until you ask.

For the SINU staff, it was when they got consistent hot water.

For another unit, it's when they get IV poles.

For others, it may be when they can get food from the cafeteria late at night.

For somebody else, it is when they get an evaluation on time.

For another person, it is when they get a thank you note at home.

And for someone else, it's when that coworker or leader who has been miserable to them for their whole life is finally asked to leave the organization.

The key thing to find out is "What's the what?" for your employees, physicians, patients, and volunteers. Because when you get enough "whats" answered, you get enough employees with you. When you have that critical mass on board, something magical happens. You have created an organization that is a great place for patients to get care, for physicians to practice medicine, and employees to work. And isn't that what health care is all about?

A FINAL OBSERVATION

Focusing on employee satisfaction is not a quick fix. It's a process. You can't wait for the perfect time to begin or measure. Conditions are never perfect. **You just have to start. You must act.**

IT WORKS!

Excerpted from a note to a Studer Group coach

Angela,

It works! While in Chicago at Studer Group's "What's Right in Health Care" conference, I took the opportunity to renew old friendships with colleagues at another hospital who were also attending. Even though we haven't worked together in ten years, the connection was still there. We were all tremendously excited to share our successes, learnings, and best practices.

After I returned home, I kept thinking about all I had said about the wonderful staff I was privileged to lead and about how much fun it was to start a new program and help it grow. So I decided to make staff appreciation a priority right away. I planned a most unusual staff meeting. I asked each individual to bring a crayon or marker as a "ticket" to enter the room. Then I went crazy decorating—as if for a party— with color-coded tables, balloons, pompoms, megaphones, food, and door prizes. I covered the walls with 44 large flip-chart pages. Each had a staff member's name on it. They literally took up every available bit of wall space!

So I began by telling them how attending the meeting had rekindled my passion and excitement for our journey. And I shared how much I appreciated each of them, including some of the stories that demonstrated their extraordinary commitment to excellence.

We talked about the importance of having the opportunity to share how glad we were that each of the people in that room had chosen to work at our organization. The team members then circulated around the room with their crayons, writing comments on each others' wall pages. There were tears, hugs, expressions of thanks.

We wrapped up our time together by challenging ourselves to continue our quest for greatness and a renewed commitment to use our collective strengths to be the very best rehab team anywhere. After the meeting, people posted their pages in their cubicles, on their refrigerators at home, and on the seat of the car to read between visiting patients.

But this was the most exciting part: That passion and rekindling that started at the "What's Right in Health Care" conference in Chicago spread right before my eyes. The comments people shared with me and left on my voice mail were unbelievable. The excitement shone in their eyes. Some stopped in to say, "Thanks for reminding us why we started in this business." Or "I really want to do this. Together, I know we really can be the very best!" and "I'm so glad I work here. I can't imagine working with any other group."

What an experience! I can't wait to see what happens next!

Becky
Rehabilitation Services Manager

- Prescriptive To Do's
- Results Tied to Each Pillar
- Self-Motivation

Principles

Pillar Results

Passion

Purpose
Worthwhile
Work and
Making
a Difference

**HARDWIRING
EXCELLENCE**

Chapter Eight

◉

Principle 6
Build Individual Accountability

The first Five Principles described a great number of actions required by organizational leaders to make the culture better for employees, physicians, and patients. The focus of this chapter on Principle 6 will be how to create a sense of ownership within the organization. It's amazing what staff will do when they feel the power of their behaviors and actions aligned with those of everyone else in the organization.

A hospital cafeteria is a great place to observe ownership. If employees leave trays on the table, they are renters, not owners.

When you check out of a hotel, do you go overboard cleaning up before you leave your room? When you have a rental car, do you wash it before you turn it back in?

Renters and owners behave differently. Our goal as leaders is to create a culture that creates owners rather than renters. As I have already mentioned, we can't motivate employees. They motivate themselves. But leaders can create a culture in which people are more inspired to motivate themselves than in average work environments. And they can avoid words and actions that de-motivate them.

MUST HAVE # It All Starts with Selection and the First 90 Days

How does it begin? A critical skill for leaders and staff is to ensure that an excellent selection system for staff is in place. I recommend you take this self-assessment quiz: If you are married, look at your spouse. Ask yourself how good you are at selection. That's the biggest selection you are ever going to make! If you are married, you've already done peer interviewing. I'm sure all your friends told you what they thought. And no doubt, your parents provided their input as well. You probably also did a little behavioral-based questioning.

In building individual accountability, we essentially ask the employee to hire their co-worker. By the time we get to Principle 6, we are saying, "We're an adult organization. Everybody has the data. We have well-trained leaders. Everyone has the tools and equipment to do the job or knows why not. Now step up to the plate."

Which means, hire your co-workers. Train your co-workers. Orientate your co-workers. Role model for your co-workers.

There may be some push back from some employees. A very few will say, "I don't want to interview. That's your job." Well, you have to. This is a co-worker. We want to make sure co-workers agree they are the best people for the job and will assimilate well within the department. And we'd rather know before we hire them than afterwards.

Some leaders will say, "What if we lose potential employees by making them jump through so many hoops to get hired?" I don't think you will lose people. I think those individuals will feel better about the organization as they meet with the employees they will be working with. It's a fair and adult way to join an organization.

We have received great feedback from hospitals across the country regarding our recommended peer-interviewing process. On the whole, the interviewers like and appreciate it. And it reduces turnover. That is why we include it in the video **Employee Selection and the First 90 Days,** part of Studer Group's Must Haves Video Series.

When employees are owners of an organization, they don't say, "It's not my job." They take people where they want to go. They hardwire such behaviors into their daily routines. They interview potential peers. They use **Key Words at Key Times** with key behaviors. They behave as an owner.

PEER INTERVIEWING: AN INTRODUCTION

We got the idea of peer interviewing from physicians. In a group practice, several physicians interview a doctor for a potential spot. That's peer interviewing. If six doctors interview a physician and one doesn't feel good about the physician, what happens? The doctor doesn't get hired. We can learn a lot from physicians on selection. They know what it costs if they don't make a good choice.

Peer interviewing in your staff is very similar. It's going to make for a good beginning. First of all, every individual who peer interviewed the new hire already knows that they can get along with the new person. Second, they're going to take a personal interest and ownership in that person's success.

I get two main objections from leaders to peer interviewing:

1. What if they hire somebody I don't want them to hire?

Don't let them interview these people. Screen people first. The leader of the department should lead the way in screening. Don't let anyone through unless you can live with them.

2. I don't want people I might hire to meet the staff they might be working with.

In other words, if they met their co-workers, they might not want the job? If this is the case, there are other existing problems in the department that need to be recognized and addressed.

SIGNING A STANDARDS AGREEMENT

The first step in the employee selection process is to ask the potential employee to read and sign the Performance Standards agreement even before completing the employment application.

APPLICATION PROCESS

Application process includes a signed agreement and commitment to the standards and values of the organization.

PERFORMANCE STANDARDS

A set of performance standards has been developed by the employeees of
_____ to establish specific behaviors that all
employees are expected to practice while on duty.

By incorporating these standards as a measure of overall work performance,
_____ makes it clear that employees are
expected to adhere to and practice the standards of performance outlined in the
Standards of Performance handbook.

I have read and understand the Standards of Performance handbook and I agree
to comply with and practice the standards outlined within.

_____   _____
SIGNATURE OF APPLICANT   DATE

We only want employees on board who agree to align their behaviors with our values so signing the Performance Standards agreement is important.

Next, we want the leader, in conjunction with the employees, to have the same shared understanding about the skill set and attitude they are seeking. We recommend that leaders and employees put together a matrix to determine the key attributes an employee should have for that particular position. This Decision Matrix captures key attributes or criteria for the position. The peer interview team will then use this matrix during the interview process.

DECISION MATRIX COMPLETED

DESIRED	WT 1-3	CANDIDATE 1	CANDIDATE 2	CANDIDATE 3
EXPERIENCE: Minimum 3 years experience in accounting, finance or health care	3	3/9	2/6	4/12
DILIGENCE: Tell me about a time when you had to work on a project that did not work out the way it should	3	5/15	3/9	3/9
INTEGRITY: Describe a situation in which you felt it might be justifiable to break company policy or alter a standard procedure	3	4/12	3/9	4/12
TOTALS		36	24	33

WEIGHTS: 1 Preferred, but not necessary
         2 Moderately necessary
         3 Essential

SCORE: 1 Very Poor   4 Good
        2 Poor   5 Excellent
        3 Fair

The matrix is important because it:

- makes evaluation of all candidates more objective and consistent;

- ensures the interview team selects the right questions for the attributes that are identified; and

- facilitates the decision-making process and avoids emotional decisions.

BEHAVIORAL-BASED INTERVIEWING

Prior to the actual interview, the peer interviewing team will select the best behavioral-based interview questions based on the attributes described in the Decision Matrix.

Each position requires different skill sets. That is why the Decision Matrix is important. Using the right interview questions will increase the chances of selecting the right candidate and choosing a high performer.

For example, how important is it to have a **creative** transcriptionist? Probably not very.

Behavioral-based interviewing questions fall under categories such as:

- Competency

- Integrity

- Flexibility

- Decision-Making Ability

- Organizational Skills

- Ability to Follow Through

- Dependability

- Creativity

There are specific behavioral-based questions listed by category on our Web site at *www.studergroup.com.* (Just search on Behavioral-Based Interviewing Questions.)

SELECTION DECISION

Once the interview has been completed, the leader collects the interview matrix and based on the objective evaluation from the interview team, the leader can make a decision.

There will always be challenges in this process. For example, a leader's top candidate may not be the top candidate as decided by the peer interview team. If this occurs, I recommend that the leader choose the candidate the team recommended. (And as mentioned, the leader should have only put forth candidates that he or she felt comfortable with initially.)

Once we have selected the right person, we want to retain them. The first 90 days are a critical time to do so.

THE FIRST 90 DAYS

In mid-2000, I was at a two-day Leadership Development Institute sponsored by an organization we coach. The topic was employee retention. At the break, I asked a leader who was being recognized for having low turnover what she did differently than others in the organization—because she had the same pay, worked with the same leaders, and worked in the same geographic location as the others did.

She said, "Oh, nothing."

This is the typical first response.

So I asked more questions.

Eventually, she told me that she met with all new staff at the 30th and 90th days of their employment. Since it worked so well, we helped hardwire this practice in all departments. The next year, employee retention skyrocketed organizationwide. Today, this organization has won many awards, including the Magnet Award for Nursing Excellence.

Since then, we have refined the 30- and 90-day process and it has proven equally effective at all organizations that we coach. We now include it as a Must Have for service and operational excellence. It makes sense for every supervisor to meet with new employees after the first 30 and 90 days of their employment.

There's something else very important to keep in mind when you think of your new employees. The employee is comparing her *first* few weeks of work with you to her *last week* at her last job.

And what usually happens to an employee during the last week?

She gets a party.

Maybe a cake.

Maybe a plaque.

And a lot of hugs and well wishes.

And she's comparing that to this new place where nobody knows her.

And there haven't been any parties thrown for her.

And she hasn't received a plaque and probably not a hug.

And very few people call her by name.

That makes for an unfavorable comparison.

That's why it's very important to have the supervisor ask four key questions in the interview after 30 days.

Question Number One: *Samantha, now that you've been here for a month, how do we compare to what we said?*

I'm asking how our behaviors have stacked up against what we said our values were when she took the job.

You may hear about a perceived discrepancy. Perhaps, for example, you'll hear about hours: "When I was hired, I heard the job was from 8 to 5. But now you're asking me to work different hours."

If the employee brings up a question, the key obviously is to listen and talk about it. It's much better to hear and discuss an employee's frustrations rather than let them fester. Then you have an unhappy employee who may quit.

It's critical that the leader not accept "fine" or "okay" as an answer to his questions. Dig deeper. Ask for specifics. The leader must also demonstrate concern, responsiveness, and appreciation for the new employee. This will also increase employee satisfaction and retention.

Question Number Two: *What are we doing well?*

It's important to move into this realm because Samantha may already have started focusing on things that are not good.

As a part of this question, I'm also going to harvest wins by asking, *"Who are some people who have been very helpful during your first days at the hospital?"* And when she names Nancy, I'm going to ask her how she was helpful. That helps me create a template for helping new employees. It also allows me to go to Nancy and tell her the good things Samantha said. Now, how does that cause Nancy to treat Samantha? Even better.

And when a new employee says, "ICU here is the best I've ever seen," and I pass that on to ICU, how is the new employee treated in ICU the next time they show up? Pretty good. The employee has just learned that when she rewards and recognizes staff, she gets treated better.

This works well with all new employees, nurses, housekeeping, and security. This also works great with physicians.

Question Number Three: *At your previous hospital, what are some things that you saw already in place that you feel could make us better?*

Ask them that question early on in their employment—before they get too ingrained in the new system—so they don't forget those best practices you can learn from. This is a great way we can benefit from past employment. Let's harvest all that opportunity for process improvement that walks through our doors.

But in doing so, I'm not going to sell out the employee. I'm not going to run back and tell everyone in the department, "Bob says we should do it this way!" That might not go over very well. Instead, I might go to the department and say, "Here's something we're struggling with. Bob, how did they do it at your previous hospital?"

In other industries, new employers make it a priority to harvest intellectual capital. If I worked at General Motors and hired someone in project design from Ford, the first thing I'd ask about is what they were doing at Ford that we should try at GM.

In health care, we have wonderful new employees walk into our organizations with fresh eyes, but we don't often ask their opinion about what they notice we could do better. Even worse, we might send the message that we don't want to know. If an employee offers, "This is what we did where I used to work," we're more likely to say, "Well, you don't work there anymore so this is how we do it here." These are missed opportunities for process improvement.

Question Number Four: *Is there anything here that you are uncomfortable with? Anything that might cause you to want to leave?*

Typically, employees bring up misunderstandings about scheduling or perhaps a question about training they thought they would receive but haven't yet. Or, they might be confused about whether they are making good progress or not—especially if they've had multiple preceptors. In any case, this is an important opportunity to reassure them.

So those are the key questions to ask at the 30-day-employment mark and again at the 90-day interview. That's how you reduce the large employee turnover that typically occurs within the first quarter of employment.

Meeting with a new employee at 30 and 90 days will encourage future communication as well as provide feedback that will help improve the workplace and enhance retention. It also hits all the hot buttons we discussed in **Rounding for Outcomes**, in terms of what an employee is seeking from their supervisor:

- A good relationship

- Approachability

- The willingness to work side by side

- Efficient systems

- Training and development

- Tools and equipment to do the job

- Appreciation

The objectives at 30 days are to establish a relationship from the outset and to get information and feedback so it can be applied before the 90-day interview. The objective at 90 days is to provide feedback on the answers to the questions and suggestions from the 30-day check-up.

You might say, "Laura, I really appreciate the suggestion you made at our 30-day meeting to put some equipment on your end of the hall. That has saved the nurses a lot of time since they don't have to keep going to the other end of the floor. The other nurses also tell me how much they enjoy working with you. Thank you for being a part of our team." That's creating a relationship.

TIP: *One hospital in Texas gives new employees a visual map that traces their first six months of employment. It tells them what to expect at these meetings. And after the 90th day, they have a celebration. The employee walks through an archway in front of all the leaders, symbolizing that the employee is now a part of the organization.*

By the way, leaders who visualize the desired outcome at 90 days—a satisfied, contributing, and loyal employee—have an easier time reaching that goal. A leader can then close the 30- and 90-day meetings by saying, "We realize having the right people is the key to having the best place to work and providing the best care to our patients. I want to make sure we are doing everything we can to assist you in being successful. We want this to be the best place you ever work."

ON QUICK WINS THROUGH 30- AND 90-DAY MEETINGS

Excerpted from a note to Pam, a Studer Group coach

> Well, the fire continues to burn! Just wanted to share with you our first win from 30- & 90-day interviews with new employees. While I knew you were right in all you said, it is so exciting to see it all really work!
>
> Little things do in fact make a big difference, and thanks to you we are charging ahead! For example, our CNO Lori met with a new RN after her first month of employment in the cardiac center, and when she asked about any concerns, she learned that the microwaves in the lunchroom would not heat frozen items within a reasonable time.
>
> No one in Administration was aware that the microwaves were "on their last legs"! So, once it came to our attention, we called Tammy, our purchasing assistant, who bought two new microwaves. Now employees don't have to use their entire lunch break waiting for the microwave to heat up their food.
>
> We included a brief story about this in our employee newsletter, asking employees to please let us know if something was broken (or close to it!) so we can repair or replace it. We also included a special thank you to Donna for letting us know.
>
> Susan
> Administrator Director

Again, physicians also appreciate being asked these questions. One hospital has had great success with 30- and 90-day re-interviews with new doctors. This has resulted in tremendous process improvement and also has harvested great wins for the staff. They also identified some frustrations for the physicians that required very easy fixes. Leaders were especially pleased to hear physicians express their preference for this hospital when choosing where their patients would receive care.

Peer interviews and the 30-/90-day new employee meetings are both methods for hardwiring the right ways to communicate with employees at critical times in their employment. They are so effective at driving results across the Pillars that they are considered Must Haves.

These tools reduce employee turnover. In fact, our experience shows that at many hospitals, an average of fifty percent of the employees who leave a hospital do so within the first year of employment. And half of those leave in the first 90 days. If you implement peer interviewing and the 30- and 90-day new employee meetings, you'll reduce that first-90-days turnover rate by about two-thirds. Peer interviews and these new employee meetings also improve quality through more efficient and better trained staff and lower recruiting, orientation, and other related costs. Two actions, multiple outcomes.

Bottom-line savings from higher employee retention really add up. In an example typical of our experience, one hospital we coach reduced employee turnover from 20 percent to 12.6 percent in two years for a savings of $1.2 million, based on an "average" hourly rate per employee they determined. The American Organization of Nurse Executives estimates recruiting costs at $50,000 per RN, so savings become substantially greater when considering just the benefit of reducing nursing turnover.

HARVESTING INTELLECTUAL CAPITAL THROUGH BRIGHT IDEAS

I have found another key way to drive individual accountability and a culture of ownership is to harvest the intellectual capital that exists in our organizations. Employees have great ideas. It is our job as leaders to harvest that resource. At Holy Cross, we collected them and called them "Bright Ideas." They can significantly impact the bottom line and drive innovation.

However, the first thing most people think of when I mention Bright Ideas is setting up a suggestion box. It is important to realize that fostering this type of innovation has nothing to do with the box (i.e., the structure of how ideas are received). It has everything to do with training the leader.

In fact, when leaders at Baptist originally visited us at Holy Cross, the Bright Ideas program was one of the things they brought back and implemented. Later, after I became president at Baptist Hospital Inc., I spoke to the coordinator about her experience with it there. I complimented her on the excellent tools she was using (coffee mugs screened with light bulbs as giveaways, Bright Ideas forms for employees to fill out, and a suggestion box). But when I asked how many Bright Ideas Baptist was getting out of the program, she said, "That's the only problem. We aren't getting many."

To receive a high volume of quality ideas, I know that an organization must demonstrate a clear commitment to training leaders on how to harvest them from employees. How to say no to an idea without saying no to an employee. How to take an average idea and make it better, or help employees focus ideas on goals the organization needs to achieve. This type of leadership training is often what makes the difference between a Bright Ideas program that fosters innovation and one that does not.

The leader is so important in driving Bright Ideas that I recommend it be built into leadership evaluations. The evaluation tool basically says to the leader, "Unless every employee in your department has implemented a Bright Idea, it will be impossible for you to get a good evaluation." You've got to prime the pump to force the action.

And progress can be incremental. At Baptist, an early Bright Idea that an employee gave us was for the lab. We saved $2,000 by reducing the size of a bag for a particular product from five ounces to three ounces. It wasn't much, but it paved the way for employee ownership. Eventually, after training leaders better, our Bright Ideas initiative worked so well that during budgeting, we planned for $1.2 million dollars in cost savings annually from the program.

One way we've found to encourage Bright Ideas submissions is to ask employees to drop their Bright Ideas in a basket in the cafeteria. Then once a month we draw out names. I recommend that hospitals budget and award prizes for the best ideas, based on a percentage of savings from the idea. For example at Baptist, I allocated $2,500 for these prizes based on the $1.2 million in annual savings they generated. We put the name of everyone whose idea was implemented into a giant drum and awarded several $50 gift certificates to the names we randomly selected. To focus employees on helping us increase efficiency, we awarded one $250 gift certificate to an idea that created a cost savings.

One hospital listed 1,100 Bright Ideas that were suggested by employees and posted them on the wall under the appropriate Pillars. Will they use all of them? No. As a matter of fact, they won't use most of them. At first, they may only implement 10 percent. But later, that number will rise to about 33 percent as employees submit more focused ideas.

Bright Ideas can make a huge difference in an organization. I've seen the difference in bottom-line results at two organizations that I led and hundreds of others that Studer Group has since coached. But success hinges on leaders.

More Tips on Implementing a Successful Bright Ideas Program

We recommend organizations hardwire employee participation in the same way as with leaders, by also telling them they must implement one Bright Idea to receive a good evaluation.

Choose someone to champion the harvesting and follow-through on Bright Ideas—someone who will actively look for best practices. One best practice that I saw a champion implement was to require everyone attending the organization's Leadership Development Institute to bring one idea for implementing under one of the Five Pillars. You can ask this at department meetings too: "Please share something that's working well in your department that could help others."

If you are considering creating a Bright Ideas program that harvests intellectual capital, here are some practical steps to making it successful:

- **Set clear goals and communicate.**

  Setting goals for ideas will help provide overall direction. In the beginning, you might want to set a goal of focusing ideas on a particular Pillar or setting a goal to have one or two Bright Ideas submitted by every employee to encourage participation. In the later phases of organizational evolution (as outlined earlier), you might ask employees to contribute ideas that will improve operational efficiency in their own departments. The former is better as a first-phase goal and the latter works best as a goal in the later phases of organizational evolution. Once a goal is set for innovation and input, a leader's job is to communicate that overall direction and plan of action.

- **Establish a process for reviewing Bright Ideas.**

  A review process will facilitate the flow of the ideas throughout an organization. You can create a centralized review process where all ideas are sent to one center, reviewed by a committee, and then distributed or assigned appropriately for follow-up. This works better in a large organization because of the ability to spread the ideas across multiple divisions simultaneously and flow the ideas to senior leaders more quickly.

  Again endorsement of Bright Ideas by senior leaders is key. At Cleveland Clinic Foundation, the CEO reads every single idea. With that type of commitment, 65 percent of CCF's 14,000 employees have submitted Bright Ideas, resulting in over 9,000 ideas in the first 10 months of the initiative.

  In smaller organizations, you may choose a decentralized review process to take advantage of the regular communication that already occurs among the leadership team.

- **Reward and recognize for innovation.**

  Recognize employees for ideas and innovation in three phases: upon the receipt of the idea; upon the implementation of the idea; and when a number of an employee's ideas have been implemented. By providing recognition at each stage of the effort, you will consistently communicate the importance of employee contributions. You will reinforce that the organization will personally reward all employees when positive, constructive change has occurred. In fact, this recognition is a part of leadership accountability. Are your leaders noticing whether their employees are submitting ideas? When they are implemented? Who is repeatedly participating? Are they tracking them over time?

- **Train leaders how to respond.**

Training leaders how to review and respond to ideas is the underlying foundation for a Bright Ideas initiative. A leader needs to learn how to acknowledge ideas and innovation with thanks. A leader should be trained in how to review an idea based on some objective measurement criteria. It's important to find ways to say yes to ideas instead of no. In fact, if it's budget neutral, might improve efficiency, or at least makes an employee feel good enough to submit more ideas, then implement it on a trial basis.

An oversight committee can also be useful in rescuing good ideas that may have been perceived as poor ones by a particular leader. I remember a time when an employee suggested that the hospital post the hours of the gift shop. The volunteer in charge of the gift shop rejected the idea because the hours were already posted on the door of the gift shop. However, the Oversight Committee recognized that the nurse's intent was to improve communication with families by posting changes in the gift shop hours on the nursing unit.

The criteria for what constitutes a good idea can be developed by the leadership group or the review committee to rate ideas based on impact, cost, timing, "low-hanging fruit," or other criteria. A leader should learn to round effectively on an employee to further discuss ideas that might have promise but need some tweaking, or to use poor ideas as an opportunity to transform a reactive employee into a proactive, problem-solving employee. Finally, the leader should learn how to reject and accept ideas and communicate those decisions in an open and fair manner.

- **Define metrics for tracking and accountability.**

Tracking ideas is a part of leadership accountability. Sort employee ideas by Pillar; understand their potential financial impact (i.e., cost and potential benefit), and determine where in the process ideas are being held up. By creating a variety of tracking methods for Bright Ideas in the pipeline, leaders will not only stay close to employee feedback, but also learn more about how the organization digests and is impacted by that feedback.

Assign someone to keep a tracking log for Bright Ideas and rotate it to other leaders. Some large hospitals actually hire a tracker for Bright Ideas once they see the impact the initiative can have on the organization. Why is tracking so important? You want to be able to guarantee employees that they will hear one way or the other on the idea they submitted within 30 days so they are incentivized to submit more ideas. The tracker notes when the employee was notified and identifies outstanding ideas that haven't been evaluated so that leaders can respond. You can also track whether they have been reviewed by the Oversight Committee, how many ideas individuals have implemented, how much money has been saved, and the organization's allocation for awards.

At one health system, employees receive a badge backer with insignias to show how many of their Bright Ideas were implemented. Visual symbols can be a strong reminder of the power and necessity of innovation. At Holy Cross Hospital we affixed a light bulb symbol on staff badges. When I was at Baptist, we did the same. In fact, when we won the USA Today-RIT Quality Cup Award, a reporter asked employees what those light bulbs represented. Every employee could proudly explain each of the ideas the light bulbs symbolized, in much the same way that someone in the military can share about the medals they have earned.

- **Launch and continuously refine with a focus on your goals.**

  Once this groundwork has been laid, a leader can launch their program to harvest intellectual capital with confidence. Over the long term, you can refine the focus of the initiative to help address specific organizational challenges. For example: "This month's focus for innovation is within the Growth Pillar: How can we increase new patient referrals from our existing patients?" or, "Let's focus Bright Ideas on the Finance Pillar this month. How can we reduce our equipment costs?"

Harvesting intellectual capital in this way is an expression of so many of Studer Group's Principles. In addition to Principle 6, "Build Individual Accountability," the tools explained here will increase employee satisfaction, measure the right things, increase accountability, are dependent on leadership training, will increase communication, and build a focus on the positive.

In summary, Principle 6 is about building employee ownership. Employees make their own decisions. And by allowing them to participate in peer interviews, asking their feedback in 30- and 90-day new employee meetings, and harvesting their Bright Ideas, we help our employees find purpose, worthwhile work, and make a difference.

EMPLOYEES WHO ACT LIKE OWNERS

Sig's Service through laundry

Sig Jones was a cashier in the cafeteria at the hospital. When anyone walked into the cafeteria, Sig's line was always the longest. Not because she was slow at her job, but because people so enjoyed talking with her, including me. Sig made both employees and patients feel good.

Sig knew that sometimes patients were admitted through our ER, and that patients might not have family to help them. She knew those patients would probably leave an inpatient stay in the same clothes they had arrived in. So Sig kept an eye out for those situations. She would take their clothes home with her and wash them and return them the next day so they would have clean clothes when they left the hospital.

People left our hospital with clean clothes because Sig Jones, the cashier, chose to make a difference. She was an owner. Sig is a Fire Starter in my life.

- Prescriptive To Do's

Principles

Pillar Results

Purpose
Worthwhile
Work and
Making
a Difference

- Results Tied to Each Pillar

Passion

- Self-Motivation

HARDWIRING
EXCELLENCE

CHAPTER NINE

@

PRINCIPLE 7
ALIGN BEHAVIORS WITH GOALS AND VALUES

The first 6 Principles can yield significant improvement within an organization. But in coaching great organizations, we have found that to sustain the gains, an organization must align the leader evaluation with the desired outcomes and behaviors by implementing an objective, measurable leader evaluation tool.

In my view, if there are only a few things you do as a result of reading this book, let one be the adoption of an objective, measurable leader evaluation tool. Then hold leaders accountable for those results.

An organization must also be prepared to reward leaders based on those results; demonstrate a sustained commitment to training and coaching leaders to achieve them; and de-select those individuals who are not achieving goals as described — however painful it might be. This is not for the meek! But to be true to our purpose in health care, we must be loyal to achieving the goals we set. That's how we create a great place for employees to work, physicians to practice, and patients to receive care.

Through my years in health care, the idea of developing such a tool was a project that was dear to my heart. I felt it would lead to better performance across the board and help leaders connect to purpose, worthwhile work, and making a difference instead of tasks and "To Do" lists.

Today, Studer Group's evaluation tool is being used successfully by many organizations around the country. While the tool is a simple one to use, it is not easy to implement because it forces senior leaders to ask some soul-searching questions:

- What are the top priorities?

- How do we weigh them?

- Which things should we stop doing or do less of?

- What do we do with leaders who are not hitting the targets?

This tool, because it is objective and focused, quickly separates the high, middle, and low performers. It makes the low performers evident and visible, which means that if their behavior is not addressed by senior leadership, then senior leadership loses credibility fast. My experience tells me that most leaders and staff already know who these low performers are. The tool just makes it impossible to avoid taking action.

Aligning Leader Evaluations with Desired Behaviors is the only Must Have that also has a principle named after it. It's that important.

▶ MUST HAVE ## HOW DOES THE LEADER EVALUATION TOOL WORK?

The Pillars provide the foundation for setting and communicating organizational goals as well as the framework for the evaluation process as discussed in Principle 1. Once the goals for each Pillar have been set for the organization as a whole, then they are cascaded throughout the organization from the division level to department or unit level to individual leader through the development of individual goals that are aligned.

Based on the organizational goals, each divisional leader sets division goals and "weights" them for each item under each Pillar. Weights differ depending on the division and leaders.

For example, in nursing, under the Service Pillar, patient satisfaction may be 30 percent of the CNO's evaluation. A division or a leader does not necessarily need to have a goal under each Pillar. The leader of risk management, for example, may not have a growth goal. The key is for the total weights to add up to 100 percent on each leader's evaluation.

Once the weighting is set, we recommend a five-point scale (1–5) to rate results within each Pillar, with one being the lowest and five for superior achievement. So let's take the CNO's evaluation under *Service* to its conclusion.

LEADER PERFORMANCE EVALUATION SAMPLE

PILLAR OF EXCELLENCE	GOALS AND RESULTS		VERY POOR POOR FAIR GOOD VERY GOOD
Weighted Value: 30%	GOALS: To achieve patient sat results of 85th PCT	>90 = 5 >85-90 = 4 >80-84 = 3 >75-79 = 2 ≤74 = 1	1 2 3 4 **5** 30% x 5 = 1.5 WEIGHTED VALUE AVERAGE SCORE AREA SCORE
	RESULTS: 90th PCT		

In our example, this organization has set a goal to increase inpatient satisfaction to the 85th percentile (compared to other hospitals) by the end of the fiscal year. This CNO may have several such goals (e.g., inpatient, ED, and outpatient satisfaction), but together they are weighted 30 percent of her evaluation.

The next step (see example above) is to take each component and put in place the five-point system. For example, a five for the CNO for this year in inpatient satisfaction is to exceed the

90th percentile for the entire fourth quarter. If they hit the 85th percentile, the CNO would get a four, between the 80th and 84th percentile would be a three, from the 75th percentile to the 79th would be a two. Below the 75th would be a one. Thus, the CEO is sending a strong message for improvement for inpatient satisfaction.

The CNO knows what percentile triggers what score on the evaluations process. There will be no surprises because she will see weekly patient satisfaction data. The CNO will then work with each nurse leader to set their goals in the same way. Leaders might have different weights and different targets to attain their goals. But I bet they would add up to the CNO's desired goals.

The same process is used for each leader, for each Pillar. Our rule of thumb is not to have more than ten targets for the entire evaluation, and if the weight is not at least five percent, it does not go on the evaluation.

How to Roll Out the Leader Evaluation Tool

In my mind, if an organization is committed to creating a culture of excellence, it must make the commitment to evaluate its leaders based on objective measurable results. This is so important to achieving and sustaining results that we only agree to coaching engagements with organizations that are willing to make this commitment. It is the first step in committing to excellence, and it must come from senior management. Once the commitment has been made, implementation timing for the leader evaluation tool will vary depending on where in its journey an organization is starting. However, I recommend that a clear plan be developed on how the evaluation tool will be implemented and driven by senior management.

For example, some organizations already have organizational goals established and simply need to connect them to the Pillars before they start the cascading exercise.

When we cascade, the goals are rolled out by senior leaders to their divisions first. Then each manager takes historical data compared to the goals that were set and assigns metrics and ratings for their departments to ensure alignment organizationwide. (Note: Hitting a goal usually rates a "3" or "4" on a performance evaluation with "5" for exceeding the goal.)

It's also important that leaders weight the goals appropriately under each Pillar and create metrics for measurement that are significant enough for the organization to attain its goals. *This is the defining moment for ensuring sustained improvement.* By cascading goals through the leader evaluation tool, the organization sends a clear message to everyone that this is not the "program of the month" or "buzzword of the year." If it's on the evaluation tool, it's here to stay. And the challenge has always been how to sustain excellence—not just create it. The evaluation tool ensures that an organization will sustain the gains.

In fact, the first thing I did when I joined Baptist Hospital, Inc., was implement the leader evaluation tool that worked at Holy Cross. In spite of the tools that Baptist had already implemented, I felt that the reason they weren't seeing significant gains and improvement in financial performance was because leaders and employees viewed it as a "service initiative." So I explained how the focus was on all Five Pillars: People, Service, Quality, Finance, and Growth, and how it created accountability through the evaluation tool.

While some organizations have already established goals under the Five Pillars, they may not have hardwired results yet by creating accountability. That's why the leader evaluation tool is so important.

Regardless of your organization's timing, it is our recommendation that a hybrid approach not be attempted. What do I mean by "hybrid"? Some organizations have tried to modify current evaluation tools by adding this objective piece to a very subjective evaluation. In the end, it just creates confusion and provides a window of opportunity to derail the process. That is why the commitment to a purely objective leadership evaluation tool is so important.

When rolling out this process, communication and training become key. Letting leaders know that this will actually help them prioritize what is on their plate is important. Senior managers frequently comment to me about their frustration that leaders are not hitting key targets. This evaluation creates the organizationwide alignment that is almost always needed and appreciated.

It is also important for senior leaders to be the first to establish their own goals and to share them with one another and with their leaders. I have known highly committed senior leaders at several organizations who have taken this quite seriously. Their senior management teams review not only their own goals but also the goals of all leaders to ensure organizational alignment.

Not only does this ensure that there are no conflicting goals, but the 1–5 rating scale guarantees fairness. And common goals will be uniformly defined.

OTHER TOOLS TO SUPPORT THE LEADER EVALUATION SYSTEM

We recommend two tools to support strong communication about progress towards goals before leaders are evaluated:

- A Monthly Progress Report, and
- The 90-Day Plan

THE MONTHLY PROGRESS REPORT

Monthly progress reports are created for each leader within the organization and support the 90-Day Plan and Leader Evaluation Tool. The reports are set up to track the same metrics that are listed on the leader evaluations. Progress reports show actual progress made toward these goals on a monthly basis.

Their purpose is fourfold:

1. They help the leader communicate results to staff who are critical in helping the leader achieve the goals. The leaders can post the reports on the department communication board discussed in Principle 8.

2. They allow the leader to communicate progress to their supervisor on a monthly basis in between 90-day-review sessions.

3. They hardwire a leader focus on results monthly (or more frequently).

4. They identify both the areas/leaders that need assistance or coaching and those high performers they can benchmark based on their great results.

SAMPLE LEADER REPORT CARD

THEMES/PILLARS	GOAL	OCT	NOV	DEC	JAN	FEB	MAR	APR	MAY	JUN	JUL	AUG	SEP	AVG FY
SERVICE	Overall Pt Satisfaction of 99th PCT	70	71	82	90									78th PCT
QUALITY	Pain Control at 75%	75	75	80	77									77%
FINANCE	Growth in Admissions by 12%	10	10	10	10									10%
PEOPLE	Reduce Turnover to <9%	10	10	13	10									10.75%
GROWTH	N/A													8.25%

The monthly progress report captures vital signs of the organization so we can take action quickly.

In essence, the monthly progress report shows the vital signs of the organization by leader. With patients, we know how critical it is to monitor their vitals. Based on the vitals, we treat. By monitoring the vital signs of the organization, we can align behavior to what the vital signs are telling us we need to do.

90-DAY PLANS

Monitoring progress is one thing, but in health care we are what I call "full-plate people." Our plate was full a few years ago, and since then some more things have been added. Somehow, that plate is always full. In fact, if you work in health care, you will always have a full plate. Once we accept that, it's not nearly as difficult to handle.

While I can't take things off your plate, I can provide you with a system to understanding what needs to occupy the most space on your plate. I find that most people in health care have too many things on their to-do lists, with no good way to prioritize them. But using the 90-Day Plan in conjunction with the monthly progress reports, you will know where to focus.

I learned about 90-Day Plans as a teacher in special education. They call them Individual Education Plans (IEPs). That meant that every 90 days, I sat down with the parents and talked about goals for the student in the next 90 days. If we waited for a once-a-year meeting at the end of the year, it would be too late. If we only had a beginning-of-the-year meeting, it also wouldn't work because there would be no way to adjust our plans based on how well they were working in practice to successfully meet our goals.

A 90-Day Plan is a tool to manage dialogue between a leader and his/her supervisor on progress towards goals and to put specific actions in place to achieve those goals. It is primarily a coaching tool, so that the senior leader can be kept current by his or her direct report and provide advice. It is also a planning tool for the leader so that efforts to achieve annual goals do not become a last-minute scramble. The 90-Day Plan also facilitates the establishment of interim goals to create results and excitement to push to the next level.

A 90-Day Plan lists the annual goals, 90-day goals, and specific action steps (or tactics) to achieve results as defined by the goals. These 90-Day Plans are created at the beginning of each quarter. At the end of the quarter, a meeting takes place between the leader and his supervisor in which the prior three months' progress is reviewed. From there, the 90-Day Plan is revised for the next quarter and the new 90-day goals and tactics are defined.

SAMPLE 90-DAY PLAN

PILLAR	YEARLY GOAL	90 DAY GOAL	ACTION STEPS	MANAGE UP LEVEL	RESULTS
SERVICE	Patient Satisfaction results 99th percentile	Increased Patient Satisfaction scores by 10%	1. Round for Pain Management.	1	Patient Satisfaction survey results

MANAGE UP LEVEL: 1 Full Speed Ahead
2 Full Speed Ahead, but let me know before you launch
3 Do not move without permission

SAMPLE 90-DAY PLAN (CONT.)

PILLAR	YEARLY GOAL	90 DAY GOAL	ACTION STEPS	MANAGE UP LEVEL	RESULTS
QUALITY	Decrease of Unit Hospital Aquired Pressure Ulcers to 0%	Decrease of Unit Hospital Acquired Pressure Ulcers by 2%	1. Monitor patient positions when rounding in the unit.	1	Percentage of Unit Hospital acquired Pressure Ulcers reported

MANAGE UP LEVEL: 1 Full Speed Ahead
2 Full Speed Ahead, but let me know before you launch
3 Do not move without permission

The format of the plan also includes a column with a rating system to help determine when to come to the supervisor for direction. Every supervisor has employees who bring too many

SAMPLE 90-DAY PLAN (CONT.)

PILLAR	YEARLY GOAL	90 DAY GOAL	ACTION STEPS	MANAGE UP LEVEL	RESULTS
PEOPLE	Achieve turnover <10% on medical surgical unit	Reduce turnover by 2%	1. Study turnover rates to identify trends	1	Retention rate of new hires by month and turnover results by year

MANAGE UP LEVEL: 1 Full Speed Ahead
2 Full Speed Ahead, but let me know before you launch
3 Do not move without permission

issues to the supervisor. And every supervisor has employees who don't bring up issues that they should before they proceed. So, to help the employee know when to seek management advice and when not to, each action step is assigned a number. This is something the supervisor completes with the employee.

For example, if the action step has a "1" beside it, the employee knows they can go "full speed ahead" without talking to the supervisor. They are free to implement it.

A "2" means to plan on implementing, but the employee needs to tell the supervisor about it. The employee should plan it, but talk to the supervisor before actually implementing anything. There may be other people the supervisor needs to talk to. The supervisor may also feel the need to double-check the employee plan before it's launched.

A "3" means: Do not do this until your supervisor absolutely signs off. For example, if you are changing leadership positions or benefits, those would rate a "3." If you are the nurse leader of the O.R. who will be changing O.R. start times, that would be a "3" because your CNO would absolutely want to know that everyone is aware of the change and it has also been communicated to all physicians. (I have found that this kind of proactive communication is highly preferred to the more usual: "Let me give you a heads up. The surgeons are unhappy.")

SAMPLE 90-DAY PLAN (CONT.)

PILLAR	YEARLY GOAL	90 DAY GOAL	ACTION STEPS	MANAGE UP LEVEL	RESULTS
PEOPLE	Achieve turnover <10% on medical surgical unit	Reduce turnover by 2%	1. Study turnover rates to identify trends	1	Retention rate of new hires by month and turnover results by year

MANAGE UP LEVEL: 1 Full Speed Ahead
2 Full Speed Ahead, but let me know before you launch
3 Do not move without permission

Ninety-Day Plans are also a great way to communicate the amount of autonomy leaders want to give to the leaders they supervise. For instance, I sometimes hear from leaders that they feel they are micromanaged. In fact, one time I spoke to CEOs of 15 hospitals we were coaching at a large system. The system had selected a broad cross section of hospitals (small, large, urban, rural, geographically diverse) to test how well the Five Pillars approach and tools would work for them.

In any case, after I spoke about the 90-Day Plan, the importance of purpose and worthwhile work, several CEOs approached me at different times and expressed appreciation that we would be working with their hospital. "I really wish you'd speak to Corporate about micromanaging," one or two told me. Since I was curious, I asked a few other CEOs if they felt they too were micromanaged. "Oh no," they said. "That's what I love about working here. I have so much autonomy." When I checked with Corporate, it turned out that those who felt they were micromanaged were getting poor results. Those who felt they had a high degree of autonomy were getting great results. So I came to the conclusion that poor results often lead to micromanaging, while great results lead to more autonomy.

The 90-Day Plan lets the supervised leader understand exactly how much autonomy they will have. And they will understand that they are, in fact, not being micromanaged across the board. With the rating system, it becomes clear that they have complete leeway on some actions and decisions and are requested to check in for approval in a few other areas so they can be successful.

Once a 90-Day Plan has been completed, the supervisor and the employee should discuss each item and action step, and assign the numbers.

The goal is to create clear 90-Day Plans. I will caution you that the first time this is rolled out, most managers load up 90-Day Plans so that it's *not humanly possible* to accomplish the goals. I saw an HR supervisor's 90-Day Plan once. I told her that if she successfully completed her plan, she would have accomplished more in 90 days in Human Resources than our hospital had managed to do since 1951.

So, let's concentrate on what is humanly possible so we can feel successful and get some good results. The 90-day work plan is a great coaching tool. Through clear measurement, it provides a regular format to discuss what an employee is doing well and which areas need development.

SUPPORT SERVICES EVALUATION TOOL

The Support Services Evaluation Tool came about in an interesting way. One day when I was at Holy Cross, I took nurse leaders off-site for a planning day since we were starting to make such great progress in our patient satisfaction results. But eventually, Rita, a nurse leader on one of the units, said to me, "Quint, every week when the patient satisfaction results come out, everyone in the hospital sees our unit is performing. In essence, we have 'skin on the table.' But for us to improve more, I need the support of some other departments that might not be mentioned on the survey or are only mentioned in a limited way. What can we do?"

Rita was right. Everyone must have "skin on the table," or in other words, "visible accountability." So I developed the Support Services Evaluation Tool that we recommend to partner organizations today. In talking to leaders of support services departments, I've found that they are just as committed to providing great support and patient care as the nurses are.

But they are sometimes hesitant to be evaluated because they worry they will only hear about what's wrong. I recognize that ancillary departments are in a tough position. When do people notice them? When there's a problem. That's not healthy for anyone. That's why this tool is so useful. Just like data from other surveys, it creates opportunity to recognize what's going well and align behavior across the organization.

Support services evaluation is a valuable tool. It allows patient care areas to provide systematic feedback to those support areas that they rely on so they can deliver the very best care to patients. It also raises collaboration among leaders to a whole new level and can raise patient satisfaction to the very highest percentile. While the service teams will make many improvements, the teams cannot by themselves move service to this degree. To reach the 99th percentile in patient satisfaction compared to all hospitals nationwide, every employee must own service, not just those with direct patient contact. Support services evaluation is a tool that will drive this kind of ownership if leaders are trained how to use it well.

HOW TO ROLL OUT THE SUPPORT SERVICES EVALUATION TOOL

There may be controversy in an organization when it is announced that Nursing will, in essence, be rating ancillary services. To minimize this, I recommend that leaders communicate two key points when explaining how and why this tool will be used.

SUPPORT SERVICES EVALUATION

Please rate each department on a scale of 1 (low) to 5 (high)
Name and Unit: Tina Cronin, 5W

	ATTITUDE	PHONE ETIQUETTE	TIMELINESS	ACCURACY
ADMITTING	4	3	4	4
BIO-MED	3	2		2
CASE MANAGEMENT	4	5		4
FOOD SERVICES	2	2		
HOUSEKEEPING	5	5		
RADIOLOGY	3	4		
LAB	4	3		
LINEN SERVICES	3	4		
PHARMACY	2	2		

Looking Good!

Room for improvement!

PERFORMANCE STANDARDS

LABORATORY	Results on patient charts by 7:30 a.m.
	Test turn around time under 1 hour
LINEN SERVICE	Weekly visit to each nursing unit
	Response time for customer requests under 1 hour

First, it can be difficult for leaders in ancillary departments to get patient and staff feedback about what's working well and what needs to be improved. Since nurses have so much patient contact, they are an excellent resource for harvesting the wins and sharing suggestions for improvement.

Second, the level of service that a nurse can provide is heavily dependent on the level of service that ancillary departments provide to the nursing unit. For instance, a nurse can only give medications on time if the medication is available on the nursing unit. In many ways, nursing is really an indirect customer of the ancillary department. So just as hospitals ask patients to complete surveys about their nursing care, the hospital appreciates nurses completing surveys about ancillary departments.

THE ULTIMATE BENEFIT OF THE TOOL

The real value of the support services evaluation tool is that, over time, it will align each person's job to how they can best serve the patient. Prior to the use of the tool, frontline staff often view their job as a series of tasks. Over time, once leaders connect the dots, they begin to view the goal of their job as providing quality patient care and their tasks as the means to that end.

For example, washing the dirty linens is no longer just a task, because serving the patient is the goal. And to achieve that requires an adequate supply of fresh linens available to the nursing unit so they are available for patients who need them. When someone asked a janitor at NASA once what his job was, he replied, "Getting a man on the moon." This tool creates that mindset—purpose, worthwhile work, and making a difference.

RECOMMENDATIONS FOR IMPLEMENTING THIS SURVEY PROCESS

Initially, there are several decisions to be made up front. These include:

1. What departments will be included in the evaluation?

2. How often will the evaluation be administered?

3. Who will tabulate and distribute the results?

4. How can we build in specific feedback for ancillary leaders?

It is important to make sure nurse leaders and leaders of ancillary departments mutually define expectations at the outset. For example, what if a lab's goal is to have reports up on charts by 6:30 a.m.? The nurse leader on a medical unit whose physicians round after 7 a.m. will think the lab is great. But the nurse leader on an orthopedic unit, whose physicians round at 6:30 a.m. or earlier, will think the lab is terrible and chronically late. So one of the first wins in implementing the tool is that leaders can finally define the same set of expectations together.

I recommend that nurses provide input to those support services departments that they feel most heavily influence the services they provide to the patient. Such departments should seek out this input from nurses. Also, it is wise to establish a rule up front that anyone who rates an ancillary department lower than a "5" must offer specific feedback on why they gave this rating. The explanation can be included in a narrative format on the evaluation tool itself or be completed by phone. If the nurse leader elects to call, he must personally call the leader of the ancillary department to discuss the rating. One nice thing about the phone calls is that they promote a habit of more direct contact between leaders to resolve issues that impact service to patients.

TIPS:

1. Ask the nurse leader to obtain feedback from the nursing staff when completing the evaluation rather than doing it alone.

2. Use the tool to improve processes. So for example, the tool might be used on a weekly basis at first, but as improvement occurs, the survey might be conducted on less frequent intervals . . . monthly perhaps. The goal is to use the tool in a way that provides feedback to leaders of support services departments on a consistent basis to improve and sustain good performance.

3. Build the survey results into the leader evaluation tool once it is in place. Ancillary departments can now have a weighted goal in their evaluations under the Service Pillar that pertains to how well they meet the needs of patient care units based on the results of the survey. This will hardwire a focus on improvement. To achieve a rating of "5" in performance, leaders must exceed expectations of the patient care units.

4. Provide recognition for results. The Support Services Evaluation Tool offers a consistent way

---

> to recognize staff who are getting results. I have
> been to hospitals where leaders of ancillary depart-
> ments have proudly posted on the wall the number
> of weeks they have received an outstanding evalu-
> ation from nursing units! Once again, we have
> developed a system where leaders and employees
> can expect continuous feedback. And much of it
> will be positive.

I firmly believe that ancillary departments want to do a great job. But we've never given them a constant feedback tool or provided clear expectations.

The ancillary report is just one way to create metrics that feed an objective evaluation tool that is tied to outcomes. While the actual metrics may differ, the concepts are the same for each leader for each Pillar, whether it's Lab, Nursing, or Human Resources.

THE IMPORTANCE OF THE LEADERSHIP EVALUATION TOOL

Sometimes I get phone calls like this:

Quint, this stuff worked for a while, but now we seem to be stuck.

Then I ask if an evaluation cycle has passed and if they used an evaluation process that was objective and geared to outcomes.

If they say no, I know that's why they feel stuck.

If you put the evaluation tool in place, but don't hold the leaders accountable, things will slow down after about seven months of progress. Then you'll get a few more months of slower movement. Then everything stops. And we begin to doubt whether we can sustain the gains. And we start to look for the Next Big Thing that will fix our organization, as I described earlier.

I believe Principle 7 is the glue that holds the entire system together and allows an organization to do just that—sustain those gains.

We have found that once the Leader Evaluation Tool, 90-Day Plans, and monthly report cards are in place, leaders appreciate them. They provide focus and clear priorities. They help leaders determine what their top priorities should be. And it takes politics and vagueness out of the evaluation process. It also moves results faster and makes the learning needs in the organization more evident so leaders can align training to desired results.

It also holds all leaders accountable for actual outcomes rather than mere effort.

RETURNING TO PURPOSE

The Leadership Evaluation Tool is just one more way to help to refocus on the reasons why we got into health care in the first place—purpose and worthwhile work—after battling years of other, cloudy issues that have competed for our time and energy. By setting clear and objective goals, leaders create a pathway to once again recognize how their actions connect to results that make health care a better place for patients to receive care, physicians to practice, and employees to work.

LIZ'S STORY

Excerpted from a note from a CNO to Quint Studer

"I never lost faith in the end of the story. I never doubted not only that I would get out, but also that I would prevail in the end and turn the experience into the defining event of my life, which in retrospect, I would not trade."-James Stockdale, Vietnam POW

Liz received a performance evaluation two years ago. On this evaluation there were numerous "does not meet expectations" ratings, which she had not been made aware of during that year, but there were no specific examples of incidences where her performance didn't measure up. Her supervisor was unwilling to modify the evaluation. And Liz was devastated by it. In fact, she kept the evaluation in her purse for two years. Then Liz made an appointment to meet with me, her new CNO, regarding the two-year-old evaluation.

Meanwhile, my CEO was quite motivated by your June 2003 presentation. He asked me to obtain a copy of the presentation, which came to me the night before my meeting with Liz. When I read it that night, I was so moved by the Vietnam POW quote that you shared.

The next day I met with Liz. She cried and did not know what could be done regarding her two-year-old evaluation. But I could not understand why it was still troubling her so. After receiving the evaluation, Liz had sworn she would do all she could to never experience such a review again. She went on to create our monthly "Ectopy" newsletter, write dozens of articles for professional journals and newspapers, and even win the Employee of the Month award in August 2003.

I told Liz that I could not change her evaluation from two years ago. Then I helped her recognize her accomplishments, which were really positive results of that evaluation. I pointed out that her desire to improve motivated many new accomplishments and successes. But she continued to struggle with the memory of that two-year-old evaluation. So I finally thought to share the Vietnam POW's quote.

We reviewed how through all his torture and struggle, he prevailed, turned the experience into a defining point in his life, and would not trade the experience because of how it had shaped him. I asked Liz if she thought her situation could be similar, in that if it were not for that evaluation, she might not have become the professional she is and attained the degree of success that she has. I asked her to consider her own personal and professional growth instead of continuing to blame her old supervisor.

She looked at me and found wisdom and peace. She took ownership of that evaluation. Then she gave the evaluation to me to throw away, saying she did not need it anymore. I gave it back to her and suggested that we go to the shredder, discard the past, and celebrate her freedom, peace, and evolved self. Together we shredded that evaluation, and to this day she remains grateful for the quote I shared with her from you.

I told Liz that God has our lives planned out for a purpose. We were meant to wait the two years until you spoke to my CEO ... who shared your words with me ... so I could share them with her.

I learned that we, as leaders, have such a gift to motivate, positively influence, and bring peace to others. That quote hangs on my communication board in my office as a reminder of the power of caring and the difference we can make in the lives of our staff and patients every day.

Quint, when you gave your presentation to all those CEOs, little did you know how you would change this employee's life and bring peace and resolution to this difference-maker...or influence this CNO's leadership style so greatly. Thank you for all that you do and the difference you make.

A Grateful CNO

HARDWIRING EXCELLENCE

CHAPTER TEN

PRINCIPLE 8
COMMUNICATE AT ALL LEVELS

D id you ever have someone tell you that if you wanted to get a message out, you had to be relentless? Well, they were right. Communicating at all levels is critical, and we can improve how we cascade information throughout the organization; the breadth and depth of information we provide; and how we connect the dots on our actions for employees, physicians, and patients.

It's easy to think we are already doing a good job at this. I remember sitting with the senior leadership team, discussing some changes we needed to make in communication, when one of the leaders said, "I don't understand why we have to make any changes in communication. I think we do a good job communicating."

I said, "We would. We're the ones who are here at the table."

I don't think we can be confident that we are doing a good job at communicating until the cashiers in the cafeteria have the same information about the organization's goals, direction, and progress that the vice presidents have.

When everybody understands what is important and what is expected of them, tremendous growth can take place.

Employees take charge of their own development and feel more fulfilled. Patients get better care. Leaders are more effective, and the hospital keeps getting better and better.

Principle 8 offers tools that hardwire communication at all levels. While Studer Group recommends a number of prescriptive ways to increase communication, here are four of the most powerful:

- Managing Up

- Employee Forums

- Communication Boards

- Storytelling

MANAGING UP: ELIMINATE THE "WE/THEY" PHENOMENON

Managing up is, in essence, positioning people well. The process of managing up will help you gain support for meeting established goals, create more autonomy within the organization, save time, and help you better control your personal destiny.

Creating a 90-day work plan, for example, is one way leaders can manage up those whom they supervise and achieve the goals above. When leaders set clear expectations for accomplishments and give clear direction on what level of approval is needed, employees become confident in their ability to meet those expectations and succeed at producing meaningful results.

When do we manage up? I recommend you manage up when things are going well; when you have good news to share; or when you need direction on how to achieve specific goals.

The reason we manage up when things are going well is to once again create that habit of focusing on the positive. This is described more fully below.

It also helps managers better understand what is expected of them. When managers tell me that their boss's expectations aren't clear, I suggest that they meet with their boss and ask the question, "If in one year from now I have exceeded your expectations, what will I have accomplished?" (On a side note: I recommend a similar question to job seekers. At the end of the interview when the prospective employer asks if you have any last questions, say: "If you were to offer me this position and I were to accept it—and in one year I am the best hire you have ever made—what would I have accomplished?" You will almost always get the job.)

If we don't manage up, we may actually be managing "down" someone else or even a whole department full of people. We may be creating a "We/They" culture.

This kind of culture is actually pretty easy to spot. If employees love their boss but hate Administration, we know we have the "We/They" disease.

At budget time, it gets even more obvious. Manager Bess comes back from budget meetings and says, "I fought for us, but this is all I got."

Or a manager tells an employee that they want to give them a raise, but Administration will not let them.

When we do this in an organization, I believe we are taking purpose, worthwhile work, and making a difference away from employees. We are dividing staff rather than aligning them. Ultimately, we are managing down leadership, and no one wins—certainly not the organization.

By managing up leadership, we send the message to employees, physicians, and patients that leaders are focused on the organization rather than on their own personal agendas. Unfortunately, leaders will never be able to be as visible as they would like to be because of their responsibilities, but you can do them a great service by increasing their visibility when you manage them up.

There are several ways to manage up. You can:

- Manage up your boss

- Manage up your staff

- Manage up yourself and your skill set

- Manage up your coworkers, other departments, and physicians to drive patient satisfaction

1. Manage Up Your Boss

Managing up your boss positions the organization well, aligns desired behaviors, helps senior leaders be more visible, and creates an opportunity for praise.

Please don't feel that your boss is being overwhelmed with reward and recognition.

Do you know where your boss's office is? Is it hard to see your boss behind the desk because of all the positive notes and letters they have received?

Does your boss have to say, "Hold on while I move some of these cards out of the way. Let's see . . . here's the stack of thank you's from the employees. Here's the pile from the physicians. Here's the heap from the patients"?

Probably not. The truth is that our bosses don't get a lot of praise. Bosses hear what's wrong and not what's right. They get a "heads up" phone call . . . not a pat on the back.

Often when I am speaking to groups of health care leaders, I suggest they sit down at the computer of their vice president or CEO and read their e-mails for a day, separating them into positive and negative messages. Do you think they are hearing a lot of positive news? If you got those kinds of notes all day long, you might be tempted to never leave your office!

So it's not just that negative news gets passed down, but it also gets passed up more than we realize. Once I was on site speaking at the Leadership Development Institute of an organization we coach, and I suggested, at the end of the day, that the 88 leaders in the room write a thank you note to their president, who had been at the organization for a very long time. After asking them to write something specific that they appreciated about him, someone collected the 88 thank you notes and the president took them home that evening.

The next morning when he came back to the session, I asked him in front of the group, "Dennis, what did you do last night?" And Dennis, who used to play linebacker for Michigan State University and did not appear to be an overly sensitive individual, said, "I went home and lit a fire in the fireplace, laid out the cards, and started reading them. And then I cried."

If you haven't taken time to write your boss a thank you note, I suggest you do so today. Be specific about what you appreciate, because it will align your boss's behavior to your own and help you control your own destiny. For example, if you say, "Debbie, I really appreciate the fact that you always make time for me because I find this to be so important," what do you think will happen the next time you see Debbie? She will make time for you.

Even senior leaders appreciate being recognized and managed up. Especially because they can't be as visible as they would like to be. I often tell health care leaders that this is just something they must accept. How often have you noticed some free time on your own schedule to go visit a department that reports to you? Not often? We're all busy in health care, and that is even more true for the senior management team.

Managing up the boss can be as simple as providing him with information so he connects with staff in a sincere way. For example, when I was leaving the office one day, a staff member told me about another employee whose sister-in-law had died. This gave me an opportunity to approach this employee and offer my condolences.

An employee was able to manage that situation up to me, which allowed me to show sympathy to the individual.

Otherwise, I might never have heard about it. Then one day, someone might ask the employee, "How do you feel about Quint?" And that person might say, "Oh, he's a machine. He has no feelings!"

Because someone took the time to manage me up, that employee would probably answer differently.

So, we learn to manage up. Once employees learned that managing up was a priority, when I would show up on a unit, supervisors and employees would say something like, "Quint, can you come talk to Sheila? She's done a nice job."

What have we accomplished? We have built trust. But I could have never done it without people helping me, by managing me up with the right information. And it is not just our bosses or the CEO whom we can manage up. We can do the same for our staff.

2. Manage Up Your Staff

Imagine that I walked into your department and said, "Tell me what is going well." And you tell me all that is going great in your department.

And then I say, "Wow! That's fantastic! Why haven't you told me that before?"

When I ask leaders around the country why they don't share the positives in their department with senior leaders more often, they tell me they don't want to brag or seem self-promotional.

I can understand that you don't want to write a note to me, saying, "Dear Quint, just wanted to let you know what a great job I'm doing. Let me tell you some of the things I've accomplished lately."

That would look like you're blowing your own horn. And in health care, we don't like to do that. But, it's not about you. It's about the staff that makes it happen for you. So put your ego in your pocket and manage up your staff.

Help your senior leaders connect with your employees, so when a leader sees one of your employees in the cafeteria or hallway, they have an authentic compliment to offer about something that is going well.

Here's one example of how you might manage up staff. Imagine you are the O.R. manager with a goal to improve O.R. turnaround time to 15 minutes or less. Your staff have been committed, improved processes, and aligned their behaviors. As a result, they have achieved that goal. You can't assume that your boss or CEO is aware of the moment you finally did it. Good news travels slowly or not at all!

So drop a note to the CEO saying, "We're so excited down here in the Surgery Department. Due to the hard work of the surgery staff, all the support departments, staff, and physicians, we have achieved our goal of an average monthly O.R. turnaround time of 15 minutes for this month. To celebrate this, we're having a little pizza party at noon for the day shift and at 7 p.m. for the night shift. I'd like to invite any senior leaders who are available to come celebrate with staff and physicians."

Now if leaders can make it, that's great. But even if not, I guarantee you that the enlightened leader will send a card or something to symbolize his or her congratulations.

Another recommendation on managing up staff: Don't be afraid to spotlight performers. Remember the seasoned CEO I mentioned earlier who created an incredible culture change by deciding to recognize more high performers? So acknowledge the winners and relish the success of others.

One way to do this is to spotlight staff at leader meetings. For example, imagine that Paul, the head of Environmental Services, has moved Yvonne, one of his housekeepers, onto the Oncology Unit. In her first four months there, the unit goes from being one where families and patients complain about cleanliness to one where they rave about it. Paul can spotlight her success by bringing her to the department heads meeting and saying, "I'd like everyone to meet Yvonne. As you may or may not know, we have really struggled with keeping the Oncology Unit clean. But since Yvonne's been cleaning the unit in recent months, we are for the first time receiving many compliments from staff on cleanliness rather than complaints. She really understands how important it is for our staff, patients, and families to feel good about the environment they work and receive care in."

Now, to really multiply the win, Paul might turn to the nurse leader on the unit and say, "Margaret, what's the unit look like since Yvonne's been working there?" Margaret, of course, says: "It's never been better." How does Yvonne feel? She feels purpose, worthwhile work, and making a difference.

A side note: Spotlighting performers is also a great way to create opportunities for advancement for good employees — which of course increases employee retention. When other leaders hear about excellent employees, they will think of them when they are looking for staff to hire and train.

So, please communicate the good things your department does. People don't know if you don't tell them. They aren't mind readers.

3. Manage Up Yourself and Your Skill Set

When a staff member is speaking with a patient, I recommend they begin by introducing themselves, stating how long they have been in the profession, how many procedures they have conducted, how much training they receive each year to stay current with new practices and technology, and certifications they have earned.

Surgeons are very good at introducing their skill sets. If you go to an orthopedic surgeon for hip surgery, the doctor will tell you how many procedures he or she has done, how often the procedure has been completed and how long they have been doing the procedure. They will not say, "Well this is the first one I have done, but I am ready to give it a try."

Use **Key Words at Key Times** as described in chapter 5 to introduce yourself and your skill set.

4. Manage Up Your Coworkers, Other Departments, and Physicians to Drive Higher Patient Satisfaction

It's also important to manage up other staff, departments, and doctors.

What does that do for the patients?

I believe it makes them feel better about their care, demonstrates our commitment to their safety, increases their comfort with their surroundings, and makes them feel more relaxed by lowering blood pressure, heart rate, and anxiety.

For example, if a patient is on his way to your imaging department, you can say, "Mr. Hinds, I see you are going down to our imaging department this afternoon. We have an excellent imaging department and a very well-trained staff." Mr. Hinds may not know where he is going exactly, but he sure is feeling a little more relaxed about the trip.

We have found that the most successful organizations have learned to manage up other departments well.

TIP: When participants attend one of our Institutes, they often ask me to suggest a behavior they can immediately put into action to make an impact. I often say:

- Tell your boss what's going well in your department.

- Tell your boss about people who need to be complimented.

- Don't blame Administration or position Administration badly.

By managing up—whether it is for our boss, staff, self, coworker, or patients—we are focusing on the positive and creating alignment throughout the organization. It's another key way to eliminate the "we/they" problem. Ultimately, we are hardwiring a focus on purpose, worthwhile work, and making a difference.

COMMUNICATING THROUGH EMPLOYEE FORUMS

One way to communicate at all levels is through Employee Forums. I find that as senior leaders, we are pretty good at making decisions (like implementing a new leader evaluation tool), but we don't always think about how we are going to communicate that decision.

Employee Forums are quarterly employee meetings led by senior leaders. They offer senior leaders a chance to communicate a consistent message to all employees and an opportunity to learn about and celebrate their workplace. Employee Forums should occur at set intervals with a predetermined agenda that is tied to the Pillars. They are usually built on a theme that ties together the session, supports the mission, and creates an enjoyable opportunity for teamwork. These sessions should be attended by all employees, with leaders setting this expectation.

Many organizations already have Employee Forums. However, often CEOs complain that participation is low. This is often the case if leaders do not accept responsibility for ensuring that their staff attend. Also, attendance will increase when Employee Forums have a structured outcome. It is a time to engage, teach, and align the staff.

Here are some suggestions for how to plan, implement, and evaluate Employee Forums to maximize attendance.

PLANNING

Set a tone that this is important. Choose a theme or key concept for the forum. For example, if your organization's goal is to become the best hospital in the country, you could theme an Employee Forum "Everybody Has a Dream." Or, if reimbursement was just cut, how about "Who Moved My Cheese?" Be sure to connect to purpose, worthwhile work, and making a difference—and don't be afraid to have some fun.

Align the meeting agenda for the Employee Forum to the Pillars. This communicates the strategic direction to the organization. Also solicit questions prior to the forum so that the CEO can share answers to the questions at the end of the session. I recommend that leaders avoid opening up the session to general questions as this can lead to a single individual monopolizing the time. This isn't fair to everyone else in attendance.

IMPLEMENTATION

Hold a session for leaders prior to the Employee Forum to educate the leadership team on information that will be presented to the employees. Promote ownership by allowing leaders to offer input and feedback to improve the meeting. Also, prepare leaders to reinforce the information and answer questions after employees return from the forums.

Another suggestion: Offer the Employee Forums at times that make it easy for staff to attend. When employees at one hospital ranked "communication" as a top opportunity for improvement on their employee satisfaction survey, this CEO started holding 30-minute "Take a Break with Audrey" forums to provide status reports on progress towards Pillar goals. She reaches over 1,000 employees by offering each forum 20 to 30 times to hit all the shifts.

EVALUATIONS

After every forum, employees complete evaluations of the forum in addition to asking any questions that were not addressed. The results of these evaluations are used to improve the next forum. They are also shared at the next Employee Forum along with questions received and leaders' responses.

Sometimes employees even express their appreciation for their leader's willingness to share information openly. In the example of the CEO above, one employee said in their evaluation, "It's incredible that you come in the middle of the night to share all of this information with us." Not only has employee satisfaction climbed remarkably at this organization, but also goals and actions are aligned organizationwide.

Employee Forums provide the organization with the opportunity to communicate information, reinforce the organization's mission, and gather employee feedback. They connect the organization back to purpose and provide a platform for supporting the staff as a team.

COMMUNICATION BOARDS

By managing up, we have (we hope) helped the staff to feel positive about leadership and their organization. At the Employee Forums we have shared organization goals and results and created a shared vision. Now we need to communicate with the same consistency at the department level so that every individual knows how well he and his department are contributing to achieving organizational goals.

I have found that the department communication board is a particularly effective way to ensure that staff get key information about the organization and their department on a daily basis. Department boards should be organized by Pillars and provide information that pertains to the Pillars.

The leader's monthly progress report should be on the board as well as more in-depth Pillar-specific information. For example, patient satisfaction results will be found under Service.

A department may post "Employee of the Month" under the People Pillar. Or a thank you letter from a patient. The employee survey results may also be under the People Pillar.

A nurse manager may post how well the department is doing in preventing patient falls under the Quality Pillar.

The monthly department budget results may be under the Finance Pillar as well as the organization's profit-and-loss statement.

What are we doing? We are saying that every staff member needs to know on a routine basis how we are progressing towards achieving our goals under the Pillars.

The communication board is a simple, effective tool that ensures all employees have access to key information that pertains to organizational goals.

THREE TIPS FOR COMMUNICATION BOARDS

1. Some leaders ask their high performers to help manage the information on the board. That way, the leader has good input on maximizing the effectiveness of the board.

2. Some organizations have their communication team periodically select and recognize the best communication board. Team members at one hospital evaluate boards around the hospital and award gold, bronze, and silver stars. Interestingly, the team consistently selects the boards with the best information content over those that have more artistic flair.

3. At some hospitals, Administration designates key pieces of information that will appear on all of the boards to ensure that all staff see the same information (e.g., information under each of the Five Pillars with metrics that show how the hospital is performing under People, Service, Finance, Quality, and Growth).

A Word on Communication Tools

When I was a hospital president, we elected to get rid of our glossy employee newsletter, which had a picture of the administration in it. Instead, we moved to a weekly white sheet of paper. It said, "Here's what's going on this week . . . " We simply called it "For Your Information." It was very factual. It said things like:

"This parking lot is going to be closed."

"We bought three blood pressure cuffs for this department."

"We just got a new microwave."

We learned that employees define quality communication in terms of quick wins on what they really need to know about. Newsletters that feature executives in suits just don't do it.

The Power of Storytelling

I have suggested Employee Forums and Department Communication Boards as two tools to share information effectively. Sometimes though, the substance of what we share can be as important as the way we deliver the information. That is the power of storytelling.

A while back, a CEO told me that a woman had died in his hospital after a long bout with cancer. He got a call the next day from her son. The wake was going to be that night, and the son asked permission for Steve, a transporter, to leave work early to come to the wake. He said one of his mother's dying wishes was to have Steve at the wake.

Of course, the CEO let Steve go. But he was surprised at the request and so did some research. When he asked other employees about Steve, he was amazed that everyone had an incredible story about an experience with Steve. It seemed that everyone, except the CEO, knew what a special individual Steve was.

For example, when Steve transported patients, he always asked them if their feet were cold. He had learned that the temperature of a patient's feet had a tremendous impact on their overall comfort level. On his own, Steve purchased inexpensive socks, which he always carried with him to put on his patients if their feet were cold.

The CEO was so inspired by Steve that he told this story at an Employee Forum. This invited even more Steve stories from employees! About three weeks later, Steve's father died. He had plans to drive to the funeral in a distant city in a car that just might not make it. When the employees heard about it, they took up a collection and bought Steve a plane ticket to be at his father's funeral.

The CEO looked at me and said, "Quint, I've realized that I have to find out who my Steves are."

Some of the best Employee Forums I have attended are the ones in which stories are shared with all staff about the heroes who are among us. If one of our primary goals is to connect results to purpose, worthwhile work, and making a difference, then I believe there is no better tool to do that than to share stories that capture employees doing just that.

But this may not happen as often as we would like. As leaders we need to go in search of them. And by harvesting them and sharing them with large groups of employees, we will hear more.

Before I visit and speak to employees at an organization, I always ask that they share letters from patients or stories with me that capture the difference their employees make.

Once I was giving a presentation to 800 employees at a hospital in Peoria, Illinois, including the management team from Caterpillar, who had an exclusive health care agreement with the hospital.

During my talk, I shared a letter they gave me from parents of a child who had been cared for in this organization's children's hospital. There was no question this young girl was going to die so the family asked if they could bring their child home so she could die at home.

But there were a lot of challenges to overcome to make this work. The family lived two hours from the hospital and the child was very sick. The nurses sat down with Home Health and made arrangements for all of the equipment to go home. The doctor said, "I'll rearrange my schedule," and rode in the ambulance home with the child—where he stayed with the family for 48 hours until the child died. Because the family was grieving, the doctor rented a car and drove back to Peoria.

As I read this story, 800 hospital employees listened in stunned silence. I could see the pride they had in their hospital. They knew they worked for a great organization, with caring clinicians, including that doctor. What a powerful and moving story of how health care provides purpose, does worthwhile work, and makes a difference!

Then I asked how many people knew about that event.

Four hands went up . . . the CEO . . . the COO . . . the nurse manager on the floor . . . and the doctor.

Shouldn't 800 people have known that story?

You see, each and every day acts of heroism take place in health care. And not just in the organization across town. These stories live in your halls and are just waiting for you to hold them up to the light. By sharing these stories, we build a culture that says, "This is what we are about. These are the acts we strive for. These are the things for which we come to work each day."

So actively collect those stories. If you create a standard of behavior, tell a story about someone who exemplifies it. One of our standards of behavior at Baptist was: "Take people where they're going." So if a visitor asked how to get somewhere in the hospital, instead of giving directions and pointing, we expected our employees to say, "Let me take you there."

At first, it sounded goofy and felt a little uncomfortable. And employees felt it might eat up too much time, making them less productive. But they felt differently when we began to share inspirational stories that conveyed employee appreciation.

I received one letter, for example, that said:

Dear Hospital Administrator,

My husband was having chest pains and was taken to your hospital. Not our hospital of choice. I drove up to the hospital and came in the wrong door. An employee came up and said, "How can I help you?"

I said, "My husband's in the ER," and the employee walked me all the way to the ER. By the time I got there, I was still concerned about my husband's chest pains, but I was no longer concerned that we were in the wrong hospital.

I read that letter to a total of 1,700 employees at our Employee Forums. Three employees came up to me afterwards and proudly said, "That was me."

While it was only one of them, all three left feeling great. Why? Because they made a difference. And they were right. Whether they helped that person or another one, they made a difference.

By connecting the story to the behavior you're looking for, you inspire.

Creating a culture of excellence is the goal. In health care today, we really can't compete on price because most reimbursement is fixed. Technology can be duplicated and surpassed. But you can't duplicate culture. It's hard to build. And it takes time. But that's your competitive edge.

How do people decide which hospital to go to? They go where their friends and neighbors have had a positive experience. As a matter of fact, the majority of health care decisions are based on word of mouth.

We have to connect our actions back to our commitment to excellence.

Like how taking someone where they need to go at our hospital—or enabling a family to take their child home to pass away—are how we live this value and commitment.

That's what it means to communicate at all levels.

CEOs from all over the country tell me that building this culture is the hardest thing they have ever had to do in their lives because they must get every employee on the same page. But many are achieving it—by managing up, using Employee Forums, keeping communication boards current, and sharing inspirational stories.

Every day Fire Starters nationwide are focusing on actions that have purpose, create worthwhile work, and make a difference through an unshakable commitment to excellence. And the Flywheel turns.

HARDWIRING EXCELLENCE

CHAPTER ELEVEN

PRINCIPLE 9
RECOGNIZE AND REWARD SUCCESS

Principle 9 shows how to hardwire the acknowledgement of great work. By calling attention to such behavior, the behavior will be repeated.

I've asked thousands of heath care professionals at our Studer Group Institutes and other forums if they feel "overly" rewarded and recognized at work every day. They usually laugh and joke and ultimately respond:

No.

When I ask that question to managers, I often announce that in a few minutes I'll be talking to their employees and I ask them to predict how they'll answer that question. When leaders hold up the mirror, they recognize that their employees will answer the same way.

I don't think we have been as good at reward and recognition in health care as we need to be. I wasn't. And I didn't take ownership for why I wasn't. I just came up with excuses. There was:

- Martyrdom. "I don't need a compliment . . . why should they?"

- Another Day, Another Dollar. "They should just be happy with a day's work for a day's pay."

- The Scrooge Mentality. "Hey! I can only give out so many compliments per week."

- Pride. "This is hokey."

In reality, people appreciate specific feedback more than you might expect. And we all know there's more to a day's work than a day's pay if we are going to stick around for a while. And if you think it's hokey, just wait until you receive your first heartfelt compliment.

Remember, too, that it is okay to feel uncomfortable when you begin to increase the number of compliments you give. If it's a new behavior, it will feel a little funny at first, but once you see the impact it has on those around you, I predict you will become a believer in frequent reward and recognition.

CRITICISM VERSUS COMPLIMENTS

As I mentioned earlier, studies have shown that our employees need three compliments to every criticism. I didn't know that. I thought it was one compliment for every criticism. I thought I heard that compliments and criticism were supposed to be balanced.[1]

But the truth is, if you give a staff member one compliment and one criticism, it equals a negative relationship.

If you give a staff member two compliments to one criticism, it will equal a neutral relationship

If you give a staff three compliments to one criticism, it will equal a positive relationship.

I didn't want to compliment people because I was afraid it would hurt them physically. Yes, I could hurt them. How?

Their head could swell up.

Have you almost received a compliment but someone else performed an intervention? They say, "Don't compliment her! She'll get a big head."

It's a myth. I've never yet seen anyone brought into the E.R. because of a big head from receiving compliments.

I even blamed my bosses. If I didn't get them, how could I give them?

Imagine . . .

Bernie: "Hi, Joe. I'm Bernie. I'm the Administrator at the hospital. You've been here for ten years?"

Joe: "Yes, sir."

Bernie: "Joe, you know why I've never rewarded and recognized you?"

Joe: "No, sir."

Bernie: "Because nobody rewards and recognizes me, Joe. You know what else, Joe?"

Joe: "No, sir."

Bernie: "They call it work. W-O-R-K. They don't call it play. You know what else?"

Joe: "No, sir."

Bernie: "You're just lucky to have a job."

But what if Bernie got some training on how to effectively reward and recognize employees so he could do things a little differently? Joe might not be a believer at first if he heard that his supervisor wanted to see him.

Do you think he's thinking, "Oh good, Bernie's probably had a personal transformation!"?

Probably not.

But then Bernie says, "Joe, you've been here for ten years and you've done a great job. We're a better hospital because of you. And I want to thank you."

Now when Joe leaves, he *might* be thinking they've changed Bernie's medication. But eventually, he's going to be appreciative if Bernie keeps rewarding and recognizing him for his performance.

Have you ever been called to your boss's office?

Is *your* first thought: "Well, here we go *again*—more reward and recognition. When are these countless compliments going to *stop*? They're killing my productivity!"

No, that's not how it happens. In fact, when I worked at hospitals and got a message that someone in administration wanted to see me, I thought, "This cannot be good. Time to do some reconnaissance work. I wonder who else is getting called in today?" Then I'd start calling my peers really quickly and asking, "Do you know what's going on in administration? Why do they want to see me?"

Of course, all of this worrying is time-consuming, non-productive time on the job. Once I got over the initial shock, I called the assistant in administration and said, "Is there anything I should bring to the meeting?"

"Nothing," she replied.

All that did was increase my anxiety. What I have found is that because people don't get recognized enough, when they hear the boss wants to see them, they immediately think something must be wrong. That's why the 3-to-1 compliment-to-criticism ratio is so important.

In fact, if you want to evaluate whether you bring enough compliments to your department, walk into the area and see what people say to you. If the first thing you hear is "What's wrong?" or "Is there a problem?" then you probably don't bring enough reward and recognition when you show up.

Even later, when I was an administrator, I still didn't understand the value of reward and recognition. I thought it was *hokey*. It was only later that I realized that just isn't true. Even physicians appreciate reward and recognition as much as staff for specific actions.

But *specific* is the operative word here. I find that broad statements such as "Everybody does a good job" just don't do it.

Everyone responds to reward and recognition. That's why it is so powerful in changing behavior and sustaining desired behaviors.

If you are a mom, you can particularly appreciate this. Do you remember potty training with your children? Of course. Some things are just hard to forget, aren't they? At our Institutes, I often ask how many women are mothers of a daughter between three and nine. Then I'll pick a mom and ask some questions along these lines:

"Hi. And what is your daughter's name?"

"Janie."

"And how old is Janie?"

"Three and a half."

"And is she potty trained-poo-poo, pee-pee, the whole bit?"

"Yes."

(By the way, I used to just ask, "Who has a child between the ages of three and nine?" and I'd find out that Tommy was six. Then I'd ask, "Is Tommy completely potty trained?" The mom would hesitate and say, "What do you mean by *completely?*" On the basis of the consistency of these answers, I have come to the conclusion that there is no completely potty-trained male in the United States.)

"So, do you remember the first time Janie went poo-poo on the potty?"

"Yes".

"What did you do?"

"I clapped." (She got excited. Janie saw Mom pumped.)

"Did you do anything else?"

"I got her candy."

"Did you call anybody?"

"Her dad."

"Did your husband talk to her?"

"Yes."

So we've got remote reward and recognition for poo-poo on the potty.

"Did you call anybody else besides her dad?"

Grandma is the top choice here.

"And what happened?"

"One time I heard her tell Janie, 'Don't flush it.'" (Grandma was coming over to see it.)

"So, Janie has been at this for a little while now. When she poo-poos this week, are you going to call her dad? Is she going to get candy?"

"No."

"Why?"

"She's learned how."

She's moved on. In health care, we have to be able to reward and recognize and then be aware of when we can change the reward and recognition as the behavior is learned and the results get better. We reward and recognize the milestones and move up as organizational maturity increases.

DANGER SIGN

While it's okay to raise the bar for what we reward and recognize based on learned behaviors, we must be careful in our hospitals about discontinuing reward and recognition. I find that when many hospitals begin to experience success, they tend to slack off right away on reward and recognition.

People will say, "Oh, staff are tired of the pizza parties, gift certificates, prizes, and thank you notes." That's understandable, but also very exaggerated. A few low performers will try to stir the pot. The reality is that once a hospital backs off on the reward and recognition, the results also start backing off. Don't let a few staff hurt others for receiving reward and recognition.

It is essential to hardwire reward and recognition. And the best way to accomplish that is to do these three things:

- Create a Reward and Recognition team.

- Implement the next Must Have: **Employee Thank You Notes.**

- Recognize and reward physicians.

THE VALUE OF REWARD AND RECOGNITION TEAMS

While ultimately effective reward and recognition lies in the hands of leaders, Reward and Recognition teams can be very valuable in bringing an employee perspective to what will have the biggest impact. Over and over, employees tell their organizations on employee satisfaction surveys, "We don't feel appreciated."

We firmly believe the most important way to demonstrate appreciation is to provide employees with a good supervisor, access to current and in-depth information about the organization, consistent opportunities for professional development, systems that work, tools and equipment to do the job, and de-selection of low performers. However, the Reward and Recognition Team can provide a valuable service in identifying other ways to make employees feel appreciated on a daily basis.

WOW! CARD

NAME *Cindy S.*
DEPT. *Marketing*
DATE 12/5/04

TODAY, YOU **"WOWED"** ME WHEN YOU *Oversaw the BKD Quality Award Billboard on I-65. It blew me away when I first saw it. You live Commit to Excellence and Communicate at all levels and I appreciate it.*

SUBMITTED BY *James M.*

THANK YOU!   DEPARTMENT *Quality Resource*

When I was at Holy Cross, our Reward and Recognition Team invented or borrowed from another organization the WOW card, a little piece of pink paper that leaders gave to employees to recognize their accomplishments. If you got five WOW cards, you received a $15 gift certificate. Now hundreds of organizations are using these cards.

Only leaders could give out the WOWs. But leaders had to be trained in how to use them since there was so much variance in their approach. Some gave them out like candy while others were incredibly stingy with them. Pretty soon, the leaders were arguing about how to use the WOWs!

One leader would say, "Susan, someone could breathe and you'd give them a WOW Award, wouldn't you?"

Then Susan would say, "Well, someone could part the Red Sea, and you'd say, 'So what? You could have done it Tuesday if you got it done on Thursday.'"

If you wait for people to go above and beyond, you never do the reward and recognition they need to be inspired to go above and beyond. Sometimes it's inconsistent. Sometimes you have to reward behavior that almost makes you sick! But you have to start wherever your employees are to move them up the ladder.

At the beginning of the WOW program, we had to virtually force some leaders to hand out the WOW's. But it quickly helped them look for and harvest wins.

My suggestion to leaders is this: Don't be afraid to recognize consistent performance. It doesn't have to be "above and beyond" behavior. It just has to be consistent. And rewarded behavior gets repeated, which just further reinforces consistency. These individuals are providing solutions instead of presenting problems to you daily. They are being good peers to co-workers. They are providing excellent service. I think that's enough to get a WOW Award.

If you only reward "above and beyond" performance, you can have too many ups and downs, and allow too much time to pass between the awards.

So when I was a leader first working on this, I suggested we bring all of our leaders into meetings about the WOW program. We presented them with case studies, broke them into small groups, and asked, "Should this person get a WOW Award or not?"

We learned that there was a difference of opinion on the awards. So this process helped us align the way the awards were given out. We wanted the leaders to understand that we didn't want the requirements for a WOW to be so rigorous that no one received an award!

We also learned that not all departments were equal. Some departments were at different levels of maturity. For example, our ER manager had very low patient satisfaction scores. She said, "Please don't make this difficult. If I have a nurse who comes in the whole day and smiles for 12 hours, I'm going to reward and recognize that behavior. Maybe eight months from now, that's assumed behavior, but in order to get where we need to go right now, I need to reward and recognize a smile."

Once we've trained the leaders and they have become accustomed to the program, we must trust them to drive the results in their areas.

Because many individuals don't get recognized on surveys, we also use **Discharge Phone Calls** to harvest reward and recognition. This has affected the culture, because it creates more passion to perform the behavior. Rewarded and recognized behavior gets repeated.

The challenge of the Reward and Recognition Team is to hardwire reward and recognition of desired behaviors throughout the organization.

This team doesn't take the place of a supervisor rewarding the staff, or a leader writing employee thank you notes. Its goal is to generate a greater awareness about the value of reward and recognition and to create a reward and recognition tool kit (e.g., gift certificates that managers can use to reward their employees weekly).

▶MUST HAVE◀ THE POWER OF EMPLOYEE THANK YOU NOTES

When I talk to CEOs a year after they have started implementing Studer Group recommendations for hardwiring excellence, I like to ask them, "What's the biggest lesson you have learned?" They always say, "The power of the **Employee Thank You Notes.**" As a matter of fact, when we studied a few years ago the commonalities among organizations we coached that were the most successful in hardwiring excellence, we were intrigued to learn that the thing that had the second greatest impact on employee retention and patient satisfaction was **Employee Thank You Notes** (after **Rounding for Outcomes**, which was first). We knew reward and recognition were important, but now we know they are absolutely critical.

Let me give you an example of what I mean. When I was speaking to the employees at an Employee Forum at a hospital recently, I asked, "How many people here have received an **Employee Thank You Note** that was mailed to their home?" Shirley, in the front row, raised her hand.

I said, "How many have you received, Shirley?"

"One," she said.

I said, "How long have you been in health care?"

"Ten years," she answered.

"How long did it take you to get the thank you note?" I asked.

"I got it in the last two years," she said. "Actually, I received it at home."

I asked her what she did with the one at home.

She got tears in her eyes and said, "I framed it."

This is a powerful thing. And every day, I hear the same thing from different employees in different hospitals in different regions of the country. They all do the same thing with the employee note they receive at home. They cherish it.

In fact, when I was traveling with the president of a large health system to its different hospitals, a nurse approached us during one of our visits. She wanted to show us the letter she had received from that same president several months earlier. It turns out that she actually carries it with her every day.

As she told him about how much it meant to her to have her efforts recognized, it occurred to me that many leaders underestimate the impact this can have in an organization. Many leaders send a few letters out for a short period of time and then stop. To many, the thought of sending employee thank you letters seems too simple to actually make an impact—or they consider it insincere—but it is neither. It is powerful.

Because we coach so many organizations, we are fortunate to hear a great number of stories about what's working. I remember one CNO who handwrote a thank you note home to a nurse and then encountered her at the mall soon after. It was the first time the nurse had seen the CNO since receiving the note. She thanked her profusely and then went on to introduce her two children. As they parted ways, the nurse's teenage son hung back (as teenagers often do). But then he walked up to the CNO, he looked her in the eye, and said, "Thank you. My mother really needed that."

And yet, when I ask audiences weekly about how many thank you notes they have received at home, 95 percent of attendees don't raise their hands.

I once talked to a nurse who had worked at a hospital for seven years. She said her two goals were to one day meet the CNO and to have someone say "thank you." We learn a lot by hearing what our employees want and need.

If you had asked me at one time if I was sending employee thank you notes to the home, I'd have said, "Yep. You bet." But I wasn't doing it well and I wasn't doing it consistently. I *should* have remembered the power that a thank you note to the home had on *me*.

The first year I worked for that treatment center, I received a little card from the system CEO. Inside the card was a flat ornament that you could bend to put on your Christmas tree. It listed the values of the organization on it. I hung that ornament front and center on our Christmas tree. I was now a supervisor, and a part of the team. Nobody had ever sent me anything like that. That card and ornament had a powerful impact on me.

How It Works

For a long time, I didn't write thank you notes. I wrote *response* notes. If somebody wrote a letter to the CEO and was complimentary about an employee, I responded with a letter. I had it down to a science. My assistant just filled in the blanks on a template.

> Dear_____
>
> Recently I got a letter from a patient who complimented you on_____. Thank you so much. I'm going to put this in your personnel file. It's people like you who make our hospital great. Thanks for caring to make a difference.
>
> Sincerely,
>
> Quint

It's a good thing to let employees know when you have received a compliment from a patient. Please keep doing it. But if you wait for a letter from a patient, not everyone is going to get a compliment. How likely is it that the CEO will receive a letter saying, "Just wanted you to know your internal auditor is the best"? Or, a family member writing to say, "I'm dropping you a line to commend the transcriptionist. She was excellent!" How many letters are you going to get about the Accounting Department?

Since you will only get letters about a small percentage of your employees, you need to create ways to thank the people who deserve to get thanked.

But it has to be hardwired. We have to build it into the system to make it happen. If you're a nurse manager, for example, and I'm the CEO, one of your assignments would be to drop me an e-mail every week telling me about an employee in your unit who is making a difference in what they're doing.

And I need for you to explain something specific they've done. I don't want to write a generic, "Hey, nice job!" note.

If I'm the CEO, I would like you to copy my assistant on the e-mail too. Then, when I get it, he or she can print out your note, address the envelope, and provide a card for me to write.

The nurse manager's e-mail might read something like this: "I'd like for you to write a thank you note to Shirley. Shirley is an RN who has worked in the unit ten years. She was very helpful to the Johnson family when their child went through a difficult surgery recovery earlier this week."

I will write:

> Dear Shirley,
>
> Your nurse manager, Richard, wrote me a nice note about you, explaining how you helped a patient and his family through a difficult surgery recovery period. Thank you for being at our hospital for ten years. Thank you for what you did with the Johnson family.
>
> You're making a difference here.
>
> Quint Studer

As you can see, that's barely a paragraph, but I've been told by countless employees that they'd rather receive a three-sentence, handwritten note than a two-page typed letter.

Let's say you're Shirley. You get that at home. How do feel about your boss, Richard?

Great.

How do you feel about the CEO?

Even better.

If I'm the CEO, I've become visible to you *even though I have never left my office.*

And if somebody asks you, "How do you like that CEO?" what are you going to say?

"He's a good guy."

Health care just got a little bit better.

Recognized behavior gets repeated.

WHY WE HARDWIRE THANK YOU NOTES

Thank you notes don't just happen.

I received an e-mail from a division leader of a large health care system who has been in a coaching engagement with the Studer Group for several months. He asked me if we might not be missing the point and creating another bureaucracy by mandating a specific number of thank you notes and asking leaders to track the number they send.

This is a common question I hear. My answer to him was this: Asking leaders to send X number of thank you notes in a given time period has an important purpose in that it standardizes a new leadership behavior: harvesting the positives. (See *studergroup.com* for recommendations on suggested ratios of thank you notes per number of direct reports.)

Requiring leaders to send a set number of thank yous in the beginning gives leaders important practice focusing on the positive until thank yous become an ingrained habit. Over time, an organization can do away with requiring a specific number of thank yous—once they occur consistently and spontaneously.

We use the tools and practices we recommend to other organizations. For example, each week, each coach sends me the name of one person in an organization we serve and explains what that individual has accomplished so I can recognize them. I send out those thank you notes each week because the process is hardwired.

I have found that if we only send notes to those who deserve them and are specific about what they have achieved, they are accepted as authentic. To be successful in hardwiring thank you notes, I recommend that you emphasize the consistent sending of the notes over the actual number of thank you notes.

Another strategy is to determine how often you think staff members should receive a thank you note at their home. When I was president at Baptist Hospital, Inc., my goal was to have every staff member receive a personal thank you note at least every four years. Based on this goal, we determined how many notes we would ask leaders to write each week. Of course, the unit leader is welcome to send a thank you note to the staff member at any time as well.

While writing thank you notes is just one part of what makes a great leader, it's an important part. So think about the systems that need to be hardwired into place for these letters to go out:

- Managers need to be held accountable for sending in employee names and the reason they should be recognized.

- Procedures must be developed to keep track of information received and actions taken.

- Appropriate letters should be sent to home addresses.

- Senior leaders need to follow-up in a timely manner.

- The cycle must continue.

EMPLOYEE THANK YOU NOTES • HARDWIRING: THANK YOU NOTE GRID

LEADER NAMES										
Critical Care: Sam Green	X	X	X	X	X					
1 E-Telemetry Connie Smith	X	X	X	X	X					
1 M-Telemetry Ray Jones	X	X		X	X					
2 North Linda Mays	X	X	X		X					
2 Main-SNF Amy Roles	X	X	X		X					
3N/Peds Bob Jackson	X	X	X	X	X					
4E-Oncology Becky Myers	X	X		X	X					

A particularly useful way to hardwire **Employee Thank You Notes** is to use the above grid to ensure thank you requests are being forwarded to senior leaders. First, write the names of your direct reports under the "Names" column. Then check off the names of those supervisors each week who have sent you a request for a thank you note to an employee. Use the extra space to capture particular wins you want to share with your supervisor.

By using this grid, you will help your leaders develop discipline until you see that the group is consistently completing this on their own. If compliance falls off, you can use the grid again. We are adults, but developing new habits comes with training and coaching. You can't coach what you don't know. So try the grid!

Of course, this takes effort and discipline, but those leaders who put the time into building an effective system for **Employee Thank You Notes** will reap the benefits of loyal and satisfied employees.

RECRUITING THE NEXT GENERATION

One of the reasons I like employees to receive thank you notes at home is so their families will see the notes. And in so doing, we recruit the next generation. When our children see leaders express appreciation for the important work we do, they understand we are difference makers. And they want to make a difference, too.

Rounding for Outcomes and **Employee Thank You Notes** are the most important actions you can take in the first three months of your journey to service and operational excellence.

PHYSICIANS NEED REWARD AND RECOGNITION TOO

Employees are not the only ones who can benefit from reward and recognition. Doctors have to do tough things every day—some of the most difficult tasks in the world.

They must tell patients that they have a terminal disease. It's got to be terrible. Doctors have to go to the waiting room and tell the family members that their loved one has died.

And all they want is peace of mind that their patients are getting good care, efficient operations so they don't waste of lot of time (which is also their family's time), input about what's going on, and a little reward and recognition.

But we aren't great at rewarding and recognizing them. They are also responsible for bringing in a great deal of revenue to our organizations. So what do we typically do to show our appreciation?

Nothing.

Sometimes when we think of doctors, we think that they don't need reward and recognition. It's not hard to find the doctors' parking lot, because the cars in it are a lot nicer than the other parking lots. Right? So, we naturally assume that some little hokey reward and recognition program would never impact a physician.

When I was at Baptist, one of our unit coordinators gave a WOW Award to Dr. Troy Tippet, a neurosurgeon.

When I heard that, my first reaction was, "Yeah, that card probably made his life worth living." I was a little skeptical. Can you imagine this neurosurgeon getting this little slip of paper from the unit coordinator?

But I found out I was wrong. After delivering a chart to Dr. Tippet, one of our nurses came back and reported. She said, "You won't believe it. He's got the WOW Award right up there with his medical degrees!" Feeling appreciated and recognized is a universal human need.

I told Dr. Tippet that I would be sharing this story. And he told me that that award did mean a lot to him. In addition to being a great surgeon, he's also a great person. He works with that unit coordinator every day, and he appreciated the recognition as much as anyone else would. I find that is true of most organizations.

REWARD AND RECOGNITION ALIGNS BEHAVIOR TO DESIRED RESULTS

One of the things I've learned about reward and recognition is that you don't have to ration or worry about limiting it. You don't have to worry if there's enough to go around. Rewarded behavior creates more behavior to reward, which creates more results—which creates more alignment throughout the organization. It turns the Flywheel.

ON THANK YOU NOTES

Excerpted from a Studer Group Institute Attendee

Quint,

I had the opportunity to attend the seminar in Nashville last week. Before I left, I took the opportunity to send a few thank you notes to folks who don't typically receive "formal" recognition through our recognition program. It took me all of 30 minutes to write the 10 or so cards. I felt good at the time and then felt even better at the seminar when you talked about the importance of thank you notes.

However, neither of those good feelings came close to what I experienced on my return to the office today! There on my desk were two "return" thank you cards from the receivers of my original notes. Each one expressed pleasure in receiving the notes, but then took additional time to talk about the folks they worked with and the role their co-workers played in making them want to do extra special stuff. Of course I am even more motivated to send my next batch of thank you notes. I guess this is what it feels like when the "Flywheel" starts to turn.

Phylann, RN, Ph.D.
Vice President

When I ask people what surprises them most about using Studer Group principles and *Must Haves*, they often tell me it's "the power of reward and recognition."

IN CLOSING

At the end of World War II, when Winston Churchill was asked what made him such an extraordinary leader, he said, "Extraordinary times create extraordinary leaders."

These are extraordinary times in health care. And while I can't promise that this book will solve every problem, I do believe that following these principles and practices will lower malpractice claims by improving patient care, attract and retain a quality workforce, create more capacity through more efficient operations, and most importantly, capture the hearts of our current workforce to recruit the next generation.

So, I do believe that, together, we can solve the health care crisis. Why do I say that? Because extraordinary times create extraordinary people. In our Studer Group travels, we meet them each and every day.

I'd like to share a final letter with you because I think it offers an important reminder of why we all chose to work in health care in the first place—to serve with purpose, do worthwhile work, and make a difference.

Dear Quint,

Yesterday I went to hear you speak for a second time. After my first seminar, I was pumped and ready to implement all kinds of programs within my department to build morale and make employees feel good about themselves. When I got back to Community Hospital, I started an Employee of the Month program within my own department, PBX. I have a department of 12, which is small, but the program went over well. Each employee would choose someone in the department who was an all-around good employee and co-worker, and the one with the most votes won.

During the month, we would recognize this person with little gifts, cards, and favors. I was hoping it made each of my workers feel great. I wondered each month when we picked our Employee of the Month if possibly they would feel it was silly or stupid or, even worse, a waste of time.

Just like you, there was a turning point in my life, a point where I KNOW I MAKE A DIFFERENCE. One of my employees who had been here just about a year became Employee of the Month. When it was announced and she received the recognition, it brought tears to her eyes. She was pleased during the whole month. Usually she was very quiet and somewhat withdrawn, but during this month, she was "one of the girls." She talked about things with her coworkers that she had never talked about before.

The moment when I realized just how much this meant to her was when she was diagnosed with cancer. It was during the month she was Employee of the Month. While talking to her husband about her return to work, he mentioned to me that she had never felt so included and proud in all her life. The job here at the hospital was a dream job for her and she really had not felt worthy of working here. She was so proud of her Employee of the Month plaque that she hung it in her living room for all to see. During her illness, she felt that she had an extended family. He said she felt loved by her co-workers. We visited her on a regular basis and called her several times a week to see if she needed anything.

About five months later, Susan, our co-worker, died. We were very sad at her passing. I personally attended her funeral with four other women from our office. As we approached the coffin, we all saw something at the exact same moment that we could not believe . On the back of her coffin, next to her shoulder, was her Employee of the Month plaque and a card signed by all of the girls in her office. At this moment in my life, I thought of you. For I had made a difference.

Ruth
Director, Communications
Community Hospital

1. 3 compliments to 1 criticism ratio, p. 232 "How can you keep a positive relationship with an employee? Inside the Magic Kingdom: Seven Keys to Disney Success", by Tom Connellan

- Prescriptive
  To Do's

Principles

Pillar Results

Purpose
Worthwhile
Work and
Making
a Difference

- Results Tied
  to Each Pillar

Passion

- Self-Motivation

**HARDWIRING
EXCELLENCE**

CONCLUSION

Over the years, I have closed many of my talks with a variety of different stories. I'd like to share two of those stories with you at the close of this book.

BRIAN'S STORY

As I travel the country talking to Fire Starters in health care, I always carry a baseball cap from the University of Illinois, Chicago (UIC), with me in my briefcase. On the cap is a picture of a flame. Sometimes people see the cap on the table and ask if it is a Fire Starter cap. It is, but not in the way they think.

The cap belonged to my nephew, Brian Fitzpatrick, who played for the UIC Flames on a baseball scholarship. Brian was pretty excited about his baseball prospects because he was going to be a starter on the team.

That December he took a trip with the team to Australia. On his return, his dad, Mike Fitzpatrick Sr., and his older brother, Mike Jr., picked him up from the airport. Brian was enthusiastic about sharing all the stories from his trip with his mom Kathy, so they went back to the Fitzpatrick home. Then he hopped in the car to go visit his high school buddies. Afterwards, he stopped by Mike Jr.'s house to talk some more and fell asleep on Mike Jr.'s couch.

At 5:00 the next morning, on Christmas Eve 1995, Brian woke up, got in the car, and started to drive home. But he never made it. Brian was killed in a car accident that Christmas Eve morning.

We were devastated when we got the terrible news in an early morning phone call. You just don't expect to hear that your 19-year-old nephew, with his whole life ahead of him, has suddenly died.

We quickly dressed and headed for the Fitzpatrick house, where many relatives, neighbors, and friends were already gathered. All one can really do in these situations is just be there and say, "I'm so sorry." The entire day saw people coming and going, sharing their pain and grief with Brian's family.

Since you can't have a wake on Christmas Day, we went back to the Fitzpatrick house and did it all over again, as more family and friends arrived from out of town.

December 26 was Brian's wake. As it began, the entire UIC baseball team walked in in their uniforms and lined up along the casket, just as a team lines up along the infield foul line on Opening Day. They stayed that way for five hours until the wake ended. Brian's Mount Carmel High School baseball cap and baseball from his first win as a Division 1 college pitcher shared the space in that casket with him.

Early the next morning, I got a phone call from Brian's dad. Mike said, "Kathy and I have been up all night talking about the funeral. We've decided we would really like you to do the eulogy."

When I am stunned, I have a bad habit of blurting something out without thinking so I just said, "Why me, Mike?"

And he said, "Brian really liked you."

Now, let me tell you what I did for Brian. All I ever did was role model what Mrs. James, Mr. King, and Mr. Fry did for me. I noticed the positive and helped him feel purpose. I rewarded and recognized his successes in small ways. It's the little things that make a big difference in a relationship. It's all about role modeling.

Well, I had never given a eulogy before. And I was to go last, after Brian's high school religious education teacher and his college baseball coach. When I stepped up on the altar, I noticed Brian's college baseball cap and the emblem of the flame on the front of it. Just 13 months earlier, I had been called a Fire Starter.

So I talked about being a Fire Starter. I said that Brian carried a flame, and I shared examples of the difference he had made. I said that Brian's flame had been extinguished on this earth much earlier than any one of us would have imagined. And I asked each person at the service to leave with a little of Brian's flame and to take it with them wherever they went. I suggested that it is up to each of us to determine how bright our flame burns.

Since then, I travel with Brian's cap to remind me of my own commitment to be a Fire Starter and carry Brian's flame with me wherever I go. It also reminds me of how quickly a flame can go out. All we have is each day, each moment to write that note or make that difference.

And that's how the story ended—until I was asked to speak at Christ Hospital in Oak Lawn (suburban Chicago) in January 1999. I thought that was the hospital Brian was taken to, but I wasn't sure, because there are a lot of hospitals in Chicago. So when I got to the hotel that night, I called up the Fitzpatrick home to tell them where I was speaking.

Mike Sr. said, "That's where Brian was taken." Then he held out the phone to his wife in the kitchen and said, "Kathy, Quint is speaking at Christ Hospital tomorrow."

I heard her say in the background, "Will you please tell Quint to say thank you to them? They were so kind to us."

Now let me put this into perspective. The Fitzpatricks were called Christmas Eve morning and told to hurry to the hospital where they were informed that their 19-year-old son was gone. They heard the worst news a parent can hear. But what Brian's mother chose to remember was the kindness of the hospital.

So when I spoke the next morning at Christ Hospital, I told them I wanted to thank them on behalf of the Fitzpatrick family for that kindness and shared some of the story. I spoke for 90 minutes and flew back home to Pensacola, Florida.

A few weeks later, I received a card from a nurse. It wasn't what I expected. It read:

> Dear Quint,
>
> I am an ER nurse at Christ Hospital. I heard you speak a couple of weeks ago and I want you to know that I was working that morning when Brian came in and was with Brian's parents that morning when they were told. I want you to know that there's not a Christmas that goes by that I don't think about that family.
>
> Nurse
> Christ Hospital, Oak Lawn

If I hadn't been asked to speak at Christ Hospital—or if I hadn't called the Fitzpatricks first before I spoke—I wouldn't have been able to say thank you and let the staff know the impact they had.

If you are like many who attend Studer Group Institutes, perhaps you've cried a little more than you were planning on as you read this book, and also laughed a little more too.

One of the special things about people who work in health care is that we've been given the unique ability to handle tremendous swings of emotions. Moments after delivering the worst news in the world to someone, we may experience a medical miracle that fills us with a burst of joy.

That's why God chose you and me to go into health care. We can handle that range of emotions. Not many people can. What a gift we've been given to have that strength to make a difference in the lives of others. In return for our willingness to serve, we receive a great gift: purpose, worthwhile work, and making a difference.

PEBBLE IN A POND

I learned how we do indeed make a difference in a most unlikely place: my daughter's wedding.

My oldest daughter got married on June 13, 1998. I found out that when a daughter gets married, especially the first daughter in the family, you quickly learn there are three S's if you are the father of the bride.

The first S is "shell out."

The second S is "show up" where you are supposed to be when they tell you to. The third S is "shut up." Of course, you get to be involved a little, but you're not nearly as involved as the mother of the bride and some other people.

So, my daughter understandably wanted to get married in Janesville, Wisconsin, because she has lived there her whole life and her husband is from there, too. But she also wanted to be married outside. Now I was cool with an outside wedding because I thought it was a cost-saving thing.

If you're outside, you save money on the hall, right? But then I learned there are also some disadvantages of an outside wedding. There's no limit on capacity, for example. They found a nice open area along the Rock River in Janesville, Wisconsin, with A LOT of seating capacity. My daughter's only disappointment was that they didn't have a gazebo and she had always wanted to get married in a gazebo. I felt kind of bad because there was no gazebo on the property.

But let me tell you, I didn't need to feel bad. The day of the wedding, a gazebo materialized on that property. But I didn't say anything the third S.

I got to the rehearsal on June 12th. It was in the church. I was a little surprised that it was in the church because the wedding was outside. Wouldn't you think the rehearsal would be where the wedding was going to be? But I didn't say anything.

Then, right before she walked down the aisle at the rehearsal, my daughter gives me some new information. She says, "Dad, I need to tell you something. The priest won't let me get married outside until I get married inside. So, tonight I'm getting married. Tonight, when everybody thinks I'm rehearsing, I'm really getting married. Tomorrow, when everybody thinks I'm getting married, I'll already be married."

That's the first I'd heard about this—at a time when I had no option but to just shut up.

Now, the next day is the wedding. At 11:00 I have to go and get my tuxedo. I had no input. I got measured. I didn't know what it was going to look like because I got measured in Florida and the tux was in Janesville.

The only things I got to pick out were my tee shirt, my underwear, and my socks.

In fact, I had always felt like a wimp telling this story until a guy came up to me after my talk, obviously impressed, and said, "You got to pick out your own socks?"

"I sure did," I told him.

I got to the wedding early for pictures. And then at 2:30, guests started showing up. A guy with a birdcage and a couple of birds also showed up. So I went up to my daughter and said, "There's a guy here with a couple of birds. Is he supposed to be here?"

She said, looking obviously relieved, "Oh good! The doves have arrived."

This is the dumbest thing I've ever heard of. This is putting me over the edge. I didn't even know they had doves at weddings. How do you know when you're at a dove wedding, anyway?

Do people say, "Let's look up! Watch for the doves"?

So I am now paying to have two birds that look like pigeons fly over my head. If these birds flew over my head at any other time, I'd duck for cover.

So I'm suspicious. I'm skeptical. I'm thinking, "This is a major rip-off."

I see the bird guy and I ask, "When do you release these doves?"

He says, "I release them when the minister says, 'I now give you Mr. and Mrs. — —.' That's when I do it."

"Oh come on!" I say. "There's nobody who looks up in the sky at that time."

When the minister says that, where do we all look? At the bride and groom, of course! If you haven't watched them the whole wedding, that's when you're going to hone in. It's close to the end.

Not me. I didn't watch my daughter turn around. When the minister said, "I now give you Mr. and Mrs. — —," I'm like a duck hunter in a blind, just waiting for those birds to fly overhead.

I also had another problem: the scripting of the wedding. The priest who married them on Friday in the church wouldn't marry them Saturday outside, which meant we had to find a priest who came up from Marion Central High School in Woodstock, Illinois, to perform the ceremony.

It was confusing because he wasn't using the same script as the priest did the night before. So I'm just sitting there, looking at the Saturday priest, under the gazebo, with the dove guy in the back, in my tuxedo, sitting in the front row.

Then I look up and here comes a boat down the Rock River. It's full of a bunch of guys in their twenties. We had forgotten that on the Rock River you might get boats. They're having a good time. They see the gazebo, the priest, and the wedding. They recognize this as a spiritual event.

Is one of their thoughts, "Let's turn around and go the other way"?

Is one of their thoughts, "Let's put it on troll and move to the other side of the river so we don't disturb them"?

Not these guys. They revved up the engine and did a few 360's in the river. Now, people at the wedding are trying to act like it's not happening, if you know what I mean. We're all acting like we're looking at the bride and groom while our eyes are rolling towards the boat. When, all of a sudden these guys just decided to cut the engine and start watching the wedding. They're probably a good forty yards away in the middle of the river. Then one guy stands up, because he's now noticed there's a groom up there about his age and he's concerned about the groom taking this big step.

So he yells, "Hey! It's not too late!"

Another guy yells, "We'll meet you at the pier!"

I'm thinking, "Obviously, they don't know it's too late because this guy got married last night."

So I'm sitting there and I'm thinking . . . I'm thinking . . . I've got a gazebo. I've got a daughter who got married last night. I've got a priest. I got doves. And now I got guys in a boat yelling. I grew up in the sixties. I'm thinking I might be having a flashback. I'd read about those.

Then the priest comes up to the gazebo and I think he's going to say, "Now I give you Mr. and Mrs. — —." But he doesn't. Instead he asks all of us, "If you take a pebble and you throw it in a pond, how much water does it impact?"

I'm not interested right now on the impact on water of a pebble in a pond. He gets down and walks around all 350 guests. When he turns around, I make no eye contact because I'm afraid that he's so interactive he might say, "Father of the Bride, when you throw a pebble in the pond, how much water does it impact?" I 'm beginning to wish I had listened a lot more closely during this ceremony.

My mind is now contemplating this question. I'm thinking about the water and the pebble. I want to ask some questions. I want to lean over to my wife and ask if he said how big the pebble was. Then he says:

"When you throw a pebble in a pond, it impacts every bit of water in that pond."

He said that when you throw a pebble in a pond, the pebble hits the water. Then that water hits more water until the pebble has impacted every bit of water in the pond. And I would have missed it.

See, I can have contempt prior to investigation. Herbert Spencer says, "The sure way to keep ourselves in ignorance is to have contempt prior to investigation." I can have contempt. I can look at things and be skeptical and make a quick judgment. I can compare instead of relating. I can bring other people down instead of elevating myself up. I can fall into the trap of contempt prior to investigation.

But he reminded me that my actions and choices have a ripple effect. He said that a single pebble in the pond impacts every bit of water in that pond.

The priest went on, "Let me tell you why I told you this story. This is a big wedding. Some of you think that you have not impacted this bride and groom, but you have. If you work with a relative or friend of the bride and groom's parents and you are at this wedding, you've impacted this bride and groom because you've impacted this bride and groom's parents." He said,

"Life's a pond. We're all pebbles. Never underestimate the difference one pebble can make."

We constantly impact people we don't even know. Before that day in 1998, I never mentioned Mrs. James, Mr. Fry, or Mr. King in any of my talks, because they were not top of mind. But at that moment, I thought of those three teachers who had made such a difference in my life.

I realized I was fortunate to have a hearing impairment, because it has helped me to become a better listener. And because I have a speech impediment that I still struggle with, I understand that sometimes a person needs to confront uncomfortable things to become comfortable. I know what it means to have challenges.

In fact, I have been very fortunate in life. I was able to teach special education and place young adults in jobs where I could clearly see what it means to an individual to do worthwhile work.

I've been fortunate because I worked at a small treatment facility and a woman came up to me and gave me a hug and said, "Thank you for helping to save my life." I felt such a sense of purpose.

I was fortunate that I ended up working at an inner city hospital in Chicago that I regretted going to. And that I was given a job I didn't want—to focus on patient satisfaction, which forced me to ask nurses what I could do to make the hospital a better place for them to work.

Then one day, someone passed me a letter to a Sister from a young man describing his father's death and expressing what that nurse had meant to him. He helped me to remember the power of purpose, worthwhile work, and making a difference. While that nurse couldn't save that father, in essence, she saved me.

Then I was fortunate again. I got to go down to a hospital in Pensacola, Florida, and do it all over again—but this time with a keen awareness about the need to hardwire the tools and techniques so they would not be dependent on a single leader or a small group of leaders.

And because of our success there, I was fortunate because more and more leaders began to call me and ask if I could help them. I was grateful because I wanted to demonstrate that these tools, techniques, and prescriptions would work in other hospitals with other leaders—which they have.

And since the inception of the Studer Group in January 2000, I've been even more fortunate, because I get to work daily with committed, inspired staff and coaches in a national learning lab, with extraordinary Fire Starters at hundreds of health care organizations who strive to make a difference every day through their commitment to becoming both students and teachers.

And because they have helped me, I've been very fortunate indeed, because I can share their learnings here with you. And I hope that has made a difference.

- Prescriptive To Do's
- Self-Motivation
- Results Tied to Each Pillar

Principles
Pillar Results
Passion

Purpose Worthwhile Work and Making a Difference

HARDWIRING EXCELLENCE

ACKNOWLEDGMENTS

WHY I WROTE THIS BOOK . . .

While I once dreamed of being a sports writer, it wasn't meant to be, with my grammar and spelling challenges. And even though I started out as a teacher of children with special needs, I moved away from teaching once I changed careers, for I was worried people would wonder what a special education teacher knew about health care.

I didn't return to my teaching roots until I started trying to effect change at Holy Cross. That's when it clicked: that to be successful, I needed to be what I'd always been: a teacher. I also found out through a number of experiences — some very painful — that I'd also have to become a good student if I wanted to excel as a leader.

Over the years, many people asked where they could order my book. When I spoke at a conference hosted by *Inc. Magazine*, they invited me to include my book on the table with those of other authors, but I had to decline. There was no book because I was spending all of my time out in the field working with organizations and hadn't yet written one.

At last, there is a book. And I truly feel that it has been co-authored by thousands of patients, family members, volunteers, physicians, employees, and leaders in health care from whom I have been fortunate to learn. They have touched me and helped my flame grow bright.

Perhaps my ultimate dream for *Hardwiring Excellence* is that people who work in health care might want to share it with family and friends and say, "Read this. This is what I do."

. . . and Acknowledgments

I wish I could name each of the thousands who have helped bring this book to life! Special thanks to my parents, Quin and Shirley, who set an example for me with their unconditional love, and to my family, Rishy, Quin, Bekki, Katye, Mallory, and Michael. Thanks for understanding this journey and opportunity to make a difference. I know you have moved around the country, had an absent husband and father far too many days.

To all the friends of Bill W. who are among the greatest teachers in life. To Mrs. James, Mr. Fry, and Coach King for being my teachers when I needed them most . . . as well as to two teachers later in life: Al Topin and author Clay Sherman, who influenced my work. To University of Wisconsin, Whitewater for helping those with unique strengths and special needs to maximize their human potential. To Cooperative Educational School District 2 in Janesville, Wisconsin, for allowing me to teach. To Parkside Lodge, also of Janesville, for the experience of what it feels like to save a life. To Sister Mary Michael and Mercy Hospital in Janesville for taking a chance on me with my first job at an acute care hospital. To Mike Rindler for telling me I could do it, early on. To Mark Clement, my former CEO at Holy Cross Hospital, for being a role model both professionally and personally. To Holy Cross Hospital for being the match that started the fire. To the Board, staff, and physicians of Baptist Hospital, Inc. and Baptist Health Care, who caught the flame and demonstrated that this is not a "program," but a way of life. Hardwiring works.

To Craig Livermore, CEO of Delnor Community Hospital in Geneva, Illinois, and the Board of Trustees at Sarasota Memorial Hospital, Sarasota, Florida, for signing on early and demonstrating that hardwiring excellence is not only possible, but also transferable.

To Sheila and Gail, who have worked with me since 1996 . . . when Studer Group was mostly an idea. And to the great coaches of Studer Group, who hop on planes each week to make a difference at organizations nationwide. To all the staff at Studer Group who support them each day and in every way. To Maureen and Margaret for helping me craft a framework that became the Nine Principles.

To Steve, who helped get this book off the ground; to Ann, for typing much of it; to Chris for editing, asking great questions and for her organization, and dedication to making this a much better book; to Bekki for taking it from Word document to reality; and to Oakleigh, who worked shoulder-to-shoulder on this book and demonstrates passion and selflessness in so many ways.

And finally, to each of you who have taken time to read this book. I look forward to our continued journey together as we make health care a great place for employees to work, physicians to practice medicine, and patients to receive care.

Resources

Use these Studer Group Resources to accelerate the momentum of your Healthcare Flywheel^{SM}...

Books

- *Hardwiring Excellence* - Quint Studer helps health care professionals rekindle the flame and offers a road map to creating and sustaining a Culture of Service and Operational Excellence that drives bottom-line results.
- *101 Answers to Questions Leaders Ask* - Quint Studer offers practical, prescriptive solutions to some of the many questions he has received from health care leaders around the country.
- *Practicing Excellence* - Stephen C. Beeson, MD, directly addresses the physician's role in living the principles that lead to organizational excellence.
- *Results That Last* - Quint Studer brings the principles that have transformed many health care organizations to a broader business audience . . . teaching leaders of all stripes to hardwire their companies with the behaviors, tools, and techniques that create a Culture of Excellence. (Coming in 2007)

Videos

- *Hourly Rounding: Improving Nursing and Patient Care Excellence* - The *Hourly Rounding* video/DVD training is an interactive resource to be used with both nursing and ancillary staff and can be used in group training or self-directed learning situations. This tactic improves both patient safety as well as patient satisfaction.
- *HighMiddleLow^SM Performer Conversations* - This video-based coaching product trains leaders to develop a method to re-recruit high performers, continue to develop middle performers, and move low performers "up or out" of the organization.
- *AIDET: Five Fundamentals of Patient Communication* - Acknowledge, Introduce, Duration, Explanation, and Thank You. AIDET is a comprehensive training tool that will enhance communication within your organization. This simple acronym represents how you can gain trust and communicate with people who are nervous, anxious, and feeling vulnerable.
- *Must Haves^SM Video Series* - Implementing the Must Haves will improve bottom-line results, increase volume and decrease length of stay, and improve clinical outcomes, staff retention, and recruitment.
  - *Volume 1: Rounding for Outcomes* - Discover the power of rounding to proactively lead your organization to higher levels of performance.
  - *Volume 2: Employee Thank You Notes* - Gain new insights into the forceful impact a thank you note can make.
  - *Volume 3: Selection and the First 90 Days* - Increase employee retention and ownership by implementing the peer interview process. Includes four video vignettes demonstrating the peer interview process planning

meeting, the interview, the post-meeting, and a 90-day meeting with an employee.

- o *Volume 4: Discharge Phone Calls* - Learn how to use discharge phone calls to demonstrate empathy, improve clinical outcomes, learn about the patient's perception of service, and encourage reward and recognition of staff.
- o *Volume 5: Key Words at Key Times* - Build positive results by saying and doing things to help patients, families, and visitors better understand what you are doing and why.

Software

- *Discharge Call Manager: Results in Patient Safety and Satisfaction* - Automates the process for making follow-up calls to recently discharged patients.
- *Rounding Manager: Results through Rounding for Outcomes* - Enables health care organizations to capture and monitor operational and performance data in real time.
- *Leader Evaluation Manager: Results through Accountability* - Leaders can enter, access, and share goals and data easily and efficiently. Automates results measurement and drives accountability.
- *Idea Management Software: Results through Innovation* - Easily and quickly accept, track, implement, and reward employee-generated ideas, and tell your staff that you value their opinions and contributions.

Virtual Seminars

- *Engaging Physicians in Your Journey for Service and Operational Excellence Webinar CD* - Quint Studer and Stephen Beeson, MD, share strategies and tools for engaging physicians. This seminar is ideal for all health care leaders, medical executive committees, medical staff leaders, and office leaders.

- *The Baldrige Award: What's in It for Me?* - Paul Grizzell and Debbie Cardello share what it takes to become a Baldrige Award-winning organization. This seminar is ideal for all health care leaders, medical executive committees, medical staff leaders, and office leaders.
- *Tool for Leaders: Rounding Virtual Seminar* - Quint Studer covers issues that leaders often experience when they engage in rounding and discusses tools that can help drive results.

Tool Kits

- *Physician Selection Toolkit* - A clear-cut strategy developed to help you create a reliable, standardized physician selection process that positions your medical group for success.
- *Hospital-Consumer Assessment of Healthcare Providers and Systems (H-CAHPS)* - A toolkit to help hospitals align their actions with the new Hospital-Consumer Assessment of Healthcare Providers and Systems initiative. While many organizations are well prepared, they may benefit from adjustments to specific practices in order to further improve their patients' perception of care.

Institutes

Studer Group Institutes offer a range of learning opportunities for health care organizations beginning their journey to implementing a Culture of Excellence and those looking to create change in a specific area.

- *Taking Your Organization to the Next Level with Quint Studer* - This hands-on session provides the strategies, tactics, and tools necessary to create a cultural transformation within your organization.

- *Nuts and Bolts of Service and Operational Excellence in the Emergency Department* - Built around Studer Group's Nine Principles® and Five Pillars, this session is designed to teach proven processes that align with the goals of your organization to achieve sustainable, measurable results.

- *Excellence in End-of-Life Care* - Learn to apply service, quality, people, financial, and growth prescriptives and specific leadership principles to strategically improve the quality of end-of-life care in your community, adding life to your patients' days when days can no longer be added to life.

- *Rural Partnership Institute* - Addresses the needs and interests of small/rural hospitals and highlights proven best-practices from successful rural hospitals across the country to improve results, increase return on investment, and maximize their human potential.

- *Focusing Nine Principles on Food and Environmental Services* - Focuses on very prescriptive tools and procedures to improve interdepartmental satisfaction with food and environmental services. The session will build on improving quality, employee satisfaction, menu services, and relationships with nurses.

Webinars

Studer Group webinars provide the latest information and tools on topics critical to health care leaders. Each "on demand" hour-long webinar is available during a 90-day period. Go to *www.studergroup.com* to see what webinars are currently available.

Speakers

Studer Group Speakers Bureau offers a variety of time-tested presentations by known experts. Each presentation is carefully customized to meet the particular need and interests of your group and is delivered by the expert of your choice.

**Information on all resources is available
at www.studergroup.com.**

INDEX

Order this eye-opening book today—and learn how to
leverage your influence to take your organization
from *great* to *exceptional*.

PRACTICING EXCELLENCE:

A Physician's Manual to Exceptional Health Care

(Fire Starter Publishing, 2006)

Expected Retail Price: $28.00

(shipping and handling additional)

Please fill out this form now and make a difference.

Name: _____Title: _____

Organization: _____

Address: _____

City: _____ State: _____Zip: _____

Phone:_____ Email Address: _____

Quantity:_____Purchase Order #: _____

☐ MasterCard   ☐ Visa   ☐ American Express

Card #: _____Exp. Date: _____

Cardholder Name: _____

Billing Address for Credit Card:_____

City: _____ State: _____ Zip: _____

Signature: _____

Send this order form to:
Fire Starter Publishing
P.O. Box 730 • Gulf Breeze, FL 32562-0730
Phone: 866-354-3473 • Fax: 850-934-1384
To pre-order online or for bulk sales, go to: www.firestarterpublishing.com.
Books are expected to ship fall 2006. You will not be billed until the book ships.

How to Order Additional Hardwiring Excellence

This first edition of Hardwiring Excellence has been published exclusively for Studer Group partners and associates in recognition of their commitment to maximizing human potential within their organizations.

Orders of this edition may be ordered:

Online at *www.studergroup.com*

By phone at 866-354-3473

By mail:
Fire Starter Publishing
913 Gulf Breeze Parkway Suite 6
Gulf Breeze, FL 32561

HARDWIRING EXCELLENCE